IDIOT'S GUIDES

AS EASY AS IT GETS

D0128929

Zen Doodling

by David Williams

ALPHA

A member of Penguin Group (USA) Inc.

For John and Audrey, who are in every page.

ALPHA BOOKS

Published by Penguin Group (USA) Inc.

Penguin Group (USA) Inc., 375 Hudson Street, New York, New York 10014, USA · Penguin Group (Canada), 90 Eglinton Avenue East, Suite 700, Toronto, Ontario M4P 2Y3, Canada (a division of Pearson Penguin Canada Inc.) · Penguin Books Ltd., 80 Strand, London WC2R 0RL, England · Penguin Ireland, 25 St. Stephen's Green, Dublin 2, Ireland (a division of Penguin Books Ltd.) · Penguin Group (Australia), 250 Camberwell Road, Camberwell, Victoria 3124, Australia (a division of Pearson Australia Group Pty. Ltd.) · Penguin Books India Pvt. Ltd., 11 Community Centre, Panchsheel Park, New Delhi—110 017, India · Penguin Group (NZ), 67 Apollo Drive, Rosedale, North Shore, Auckland 1311, New Zealand (a division of Pearson New Zealand Ltd.) · Penguin Books (South Africa) (Pty.) Ltd., 24 Sturdee Avenue, Rosebank, Johannesburg 2196, South Africa · Penguin Books Ltd., Registered Offices: 80 Strand, London WC2R 0RL, England

Copyright © 2015 by Penguin Group (USA) Inc.

IDIOT'S GUIDES and Design are trademarks of Penguin Group (USA) Inc.

International Standard Book Number: 978-1-61564-757-6
Library of Congress Catalog Card Number: 2014954040

17   16   15   8   7   6   5   4   3   2   1

Interpretation of the printing code: The rightmost number of the first series of numbers is the year of the book's printing; the rightmost number of the second series of numbers is the number of the book's printing. For example, a printing code of 15-1 shows that the first printing occurred in 2015.

Printed in China

Note: This publication contains the opinions and ideas of its author. It is intended to provide helpful and informative material on the subject matter covered. It is sold with the understanding that the author and publisher are not engaged in rendering professional services in the book. If the reader requires personal assistance or advice, a competent professional should be consulted. The author and publisher specifically disclaim any responsibility for any liability, loss, or risk, personal or otherwise, which is incurred as a consequence, directly or indirectly, of the use and application of any of the contents of this book.

Most Alpha books are available at special quantity discounts for bulk purchases for sales promotions, premiums, fund-raising, or educational use. Special books, or book excerpts, can also be created to fit specific needs. For details, write: Special Markets, Alpha Books, 375 Hudson Street, New York, NY 10014.

PUBLISHER:
Mike Sanders

EXECUTIVE MANAGING EDITOR:
Billy Fields

EXECUTIVE ACQUISITIONS EDITOR:
Lori Cates Hand

DEVELOPMENT EDITORIAL SUPERVISOR:
Christy Wagner

SENIOR DESIGNER:
Rebecca Batchelor

PRODUCTION EDITOR:
Jana M. Stefanciosa

INDEXER:
Heather McNeill

LAYOUT TECHNICIAN:
Brian Massey

PROOFREADER:
Cate Schwenk

CONTENTS

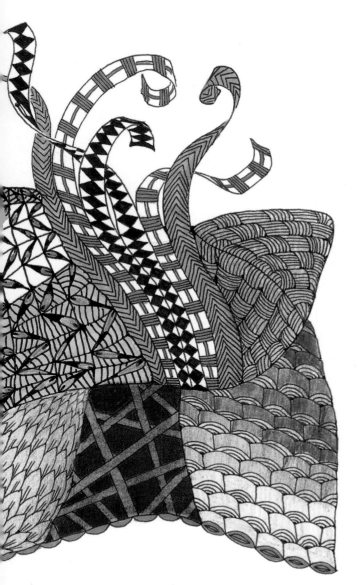

CONTENTS

INTRODUCTION

Doodles are informal drawings, but the array of styles and correlations is wide. Some are intricate and labored; some consist of shaded textures; some contain patterns; others include recognizable figurative elements. Zen doodling, which originates neither in Zen Buddhism nor in the informality of most doodling done in general, borrows from all these things and refines them into a captivating, contemplative form of drawing. Zen doodling is fairly easy to learn, even for the novice, and it's fun.

A Zen doodle is made mostly by repeating patterns, ranging from simple to complex, each with a distinctive texture and tonal quality that adds to the overall effect. Sometimes the goal of attaining a mindful state is linked to the process of its creation, which accounts for the *Zen* part of the name. Traditionally, with Zen, you aspire to higher mental focus by emptying your mind of daily concerns through meditation. The Zentangle® method is a kind of Zen doodling that engages this aspect of mindfulness along with special pattern units, called *tangles,* and by beginning with a spontaneous penciled line called a *string.* Zen doodling may resemble that process, but it includes an even more eclectic range of patterns, methods, and results.

This book presents some possibilities of what a Zen doodle can be. I illustrate the basic aspects of the art form and the underlying design principles as well as strategies for creativity. I give you some common building blocks, explore using tone and color, and present the various ways to create a Zen doodle in simple, step-by-step lessons, with examples ranging from easy to more difficult. As you travel through the pages of this book, build your understanding of the various methods by following the instructions, but also challenge yourself to create your own doodles based on what you learn here. Zen doodles are full of twists, turns, and complications, and each one is unique. Start one and follow it all the way to completion. When you reach a critical point, you might be tempted to give up, but don't. Instead, take a break and come back to it later to see where you want to go next. Each Zen doodle is a journey to surprising and sometimes curious designs. I give you a foundation in these pages; only you know where your creativity might take you.

An important aspect of this kind of drawing is the pace at which you make the lines. Begin drawing slowly to get a feel for the shapes and the speed required to make them. If you draw slowly enough that your lines possess a wavering quality, speed up a little to smooth them out. Avoid using a ruler to draw straight lines; ruled lines stand out in a distracting way in a mostly hand-drawn image, while the unpredictable nature of freehand lines adds energy and life to a drawing. In areas that require more exactness, such as circles and complex patterns based on grids, lightly pencil in the shape contours or the vertical and horizontal structure first and erase them later if they're still visible.

If you make mistakes as you doodle, build them into your drawings. Camouflage a stray mark by surrounding it with similar marks that transition into something else. Or alter goofs into something less conspicuous with a few well-placed accents. If you're not sure what to do with mistakes, consider them from different angles to decide how to work them in. "Mistakes" can be the necessary impetus pushing you to see things in a new way—and ultimately—to greater creativity.

Deeper than words, the language of the heart and soul is likely formed with color and shape. Zen doodling utilizes that language to suggest meaning with its seas of spilled-out patterns and its stretches of stippling, star shapes, and strands. Each doodle is a voyage to a far-off land with fascinating flora and fauna. At the tip of your pen, the whole exotic trip happens in mere moments. My hope is that you rekindle your creativity, one pen-powered journey at a time.

ONLINE EXTRAS

Sometimes it helps to have a head start. At idiotsguides.com/zendoodling, we've shared several of the blank contours shown throughout the book, as well as several new ones, you can download, print, and use as a starting point for your own doodles.

ACKNOWLEDGMENTS

The steps taken to write this book were sometimes set down cautiously, while others ticked by at a marathon pace. They've led to a soaring view that was possible only through combined effort. My family, Rachel and Seth, supplied love, patience, and pragmatism, and found the delicate balance between encouragement and steering clear. Chris, Cheryl, and Roger, as always, were a ready technical resource for all things rational, scientific, and mathematical. My students and friends were steadfast and provided great feedback and necessary fits of laughter. And Lori, Christy, and Becky, you gave me this space to fill and helped me fill it with the very best. Many thanks.

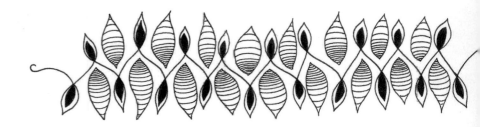

1

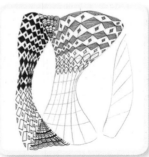

GETTING STARTED

In Zen doodling, you manipulate patterns and shapes while drawing. The process is easy: choose and draw a main shape; divide it into sections; and in each section, repeat simple shapes to create a pattern.

DOODLING AND ART

When you make a Zen doodle, your goal should not be to create a work of art. That imposing task will only produce fear. Instead, simply draw and reflect on what you're doing.

The process of drawing the repeating parts of a Zen doodle creates a rhythm that helps the critical voice inside your mind to quiet while life concerns float away. In this freed-up space, creativity begins to grow.

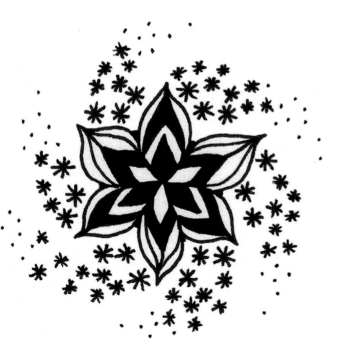

Freedom allows you to take risks without fear of criticism. Because your doodle isn't planned to be an edited and logical expression, the illusions can develop without the self-criticism that often accompanies creativity. The somewhat random bits and pieces are thought-provoking and inspire multiple interpretations. A Zen doodle is a balance of not only *what* is depicted but *how* it's drawn.

THE FOCUSED MIND

The ritual of drawing begins before your pen ever touches the paper. You must first prepare your drawing space as well as prepare your mind.

To avoid unnecessary neck strain as you draw, angle your drawing surface, whether it's a lap desk, a board leaning on a table or against a stack of books, or a drafting table, so it's almost perpendicular to your line of sight. Light your drawing surface with a drafting lamp on the opposite side as your drawing hand or with some other source or other light source to produce even lighting.

To clear and focus your mind before you begin to doodle, try this process:

1.   Find a quiet place, maybe with soothing instrumental music playing.

2.   Sit in a comfortable chair with your feet on the floor and your lower back supported.

3.   Relax until the rhythm of your breathing is steady, breathing through your nose with a relaxed jaw, if possible. (These considerations can be awkward at first, but you'll refine them naturally with practice.)

4.   Consider what you're doing. As you do, concerns will be clouding your focus and calling you to stop or to hurry up and get it done. Just remember that when you're creating, you're not working for acclaim. You're working to reclaim an important part of yourself—your creativity.

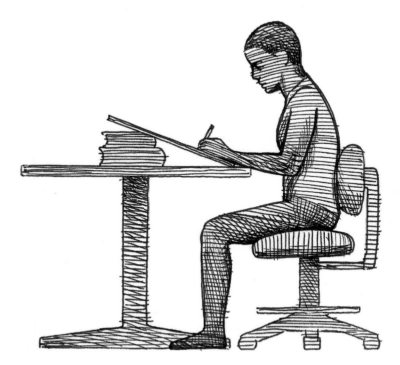

HELPFUL TOOLS AND MATERIALS

The only things you need to create a Zen doodle are a drawing pen and a piece of paper. However, incorporating various media into your doodles might inspire you to create exciting new doodle designs. Following are some other helpful tools and materials you might want to check out as you progress with your work. They're not essential by any means, but they might inspire you to take your doodling further.

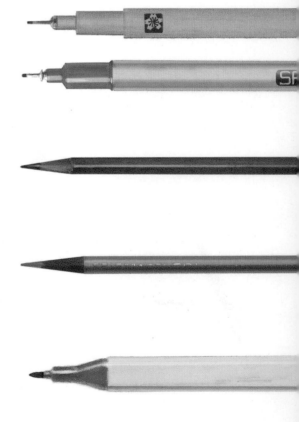

Black ink pen   Copic Multiliner dries fast; I use sizes 0.5, 0.3, and 0.1. Or try Sakura Pigma Micron, sizes 05, 03, and 01. For a nondisposable pen, try the Copic Multiliner SP, size 0.5 and smaller, with replaceable ink cartridges and tips.

Graphite drawing pencil   Many sharpenable wood-bound pencils are available. Look for an HB grade Sanford, Prismacolor, Derwent, KOH-I-NOOR HARDTMUTH, or Tombow Mono.

Colored pencils   Prismacolor Premier or Faber-Castell's Albrecht Dürer Watercolour Pencils are great for shading.

Markers   These have a watercolor effect.

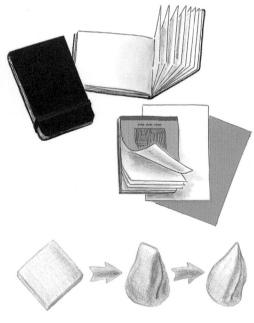

Sketchbook or paper For a sketchbook, look for a Strathmore Drawing, Canson Drawing, or Moleskine Art Plus Sketch Album. For paper, Strathmore Bristol is a good, heavyweight drawing surface for pencil and pen. Also try Canson En-Tout-Cas, or Fabriano Classico.

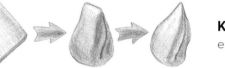

Kneaded rubber eraser Sanford or Prismacolor brand erasers work well.

Metal ruler Opt for an 18-inch (45cm) one.

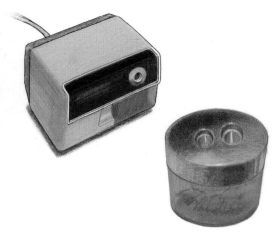

Pencil sharpener I use an older model electric Panasonic Auto-Stop pencil sharpener that works great and exposes a lot of lead. Or try the inexpensive handheld Staedtler 2-hole sharpener.

BASIC METHOD

One goal to set for yourself as you Zen doodle is to develop a steady pace that will give your drawing a unified quality. In this section, I give you a rough outline of the process you can follow and customize to help when creating your doodles.

Throughout the book, I use specific terms to refer to certain parts of each Zen doodle. Here's what they mean:

main shape   The overall shape of a doodle.

section   A smaller shape within a doodle's main shape.

construction   Light pencil marks drawn to determine placement before using ink.

contour   A line that defines the outside edge of a shape.

cross-contour   A line that travels across the interior of a shape and describes the surface.

unit   A stroke or shape that repeats as part of a motif.

motif   A repeating part in a pattern.

pattern   A set of repeating lines, shapes, and shading that create a unified visual effect.

value pattern   The arrangement of light and dark areas in a design.

tangle   A Zentangle term for pattern.

BEGIN WITH THE MAIN SHAPE

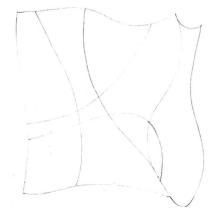

When you're ready and focused, begin with a light sketch of the main shape using a well-sharpened HB grade graphite pencil. Divide the main shape into several smaller irregular shapes, or sections, by drawing wavering and curving lines that span the shape diagonally from the top edge to the bottom and from the left edge to the right.

Make shapes that are fairly simple; when you add the tangles later, the drawing will become more intricate. As you pencil in the construction, proceed slowly and use light lines.

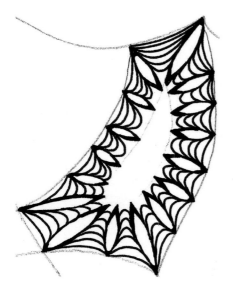

ADD PATTERNS

Now consider patterns to fit into the sections. Choose one of the more striking sections of your construction drawing, and fill it with the strongest pattern. Distort it to fit the section shape by making it smaller to fit tight areas, and customize the shapes to flow with the overall design. Fill all the sections. Transition some sections gradually into another, and maintain the borders of others.

Squint at your work occasionally to better see the dark and light values. This helps you determine if they have a pleasing pattern. Turn your paper 45, 90, or 180 degrees to assess the balance of the shapes and developing sections and to position the page to make drawing some lines easier.

Take short breaks as you fill in patterns so you can maintain a consistent level of focus. Work at a pace that's neither rushed nor hesitant.

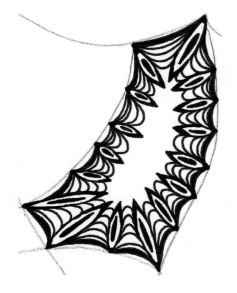

REFINE THE BALANCE

When you've filled all the sections, assess the doodle's balance of shapes and values. At this time, you can darken a pattern's overall value by adding a dot or mark in the center of repeating shapes, or you can shade corners to add more black contrast. To de-emphasize an awkwardly balanced main shape or to soften one that's too hard-edged, build out with more of one pattern, or add a dynamic border pattern.

KEEPING A SKETCHBOOK

Just as it's important to have a ready area for drawing, you also should keep a sketchbook handy in which you can doodle and record ideas for future doodles. Think of it as a mobile studio where you can freely invent and store important drawing information.

You can keep it in a journal format with entry dates and customize it with a table of contents and page numbers. Or you can use it as a blank palette to fill with your creations.

It's key that your sketchbook be easy to transport so you can take it with you and draw whenever inspiration hits. Choose a book whose pages lay flat and aren't too textured to allow for detailed pen work. And opt for one that's lightweight and easy for you to hold while you're standing, such as a 5×8 inch (13×21cm) blank-page Moleskine or other brand journal. Some books have thicker pages for watercolors, so be sure to pick one that fits your needs.

If you can, buy a separate sketchbook just for recording motifs and tangles. Draw them carefully, label them, and add your observations. This can be a great place for your own inventions as well.

Get in the habit of taking your sketchbook and a pen with you wherever you go. If you have any downtime, you can open it and draw—a creative and calming alternative to checking Facebook on your phone.

Above all, your sketchbook should be a ready place where you can both doodle and return to for inspiration.

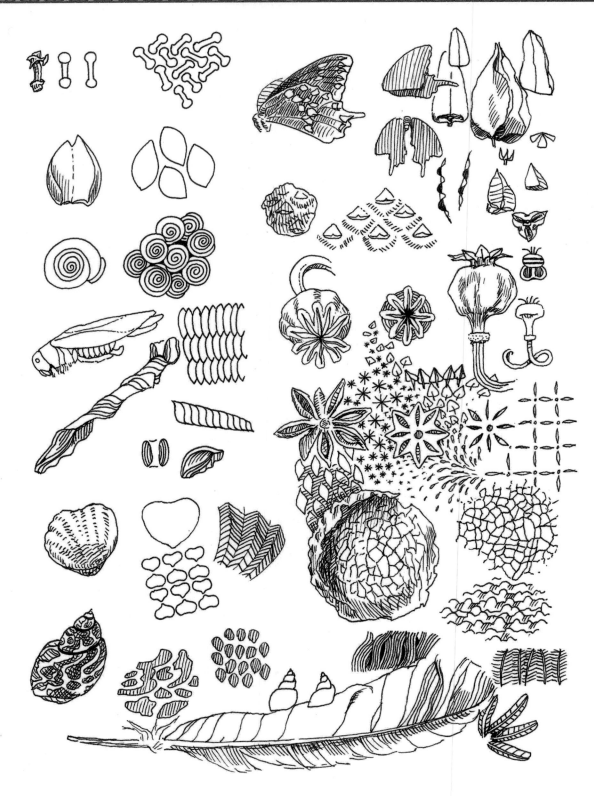

2

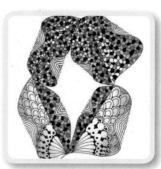

DESIGN

A Zen doodle is a balance of tonal textures and the principles of design. You can create visual interest with emphasis, unity, variety, contrast, levels of interest, illusion of depth, and a visual path.

FIRST STROKES

❧

Before you begin creating a doodle, you can practice drawing loops, triangles, and squares on a separate piece of paper to warm up. Warming up helps prepare your mind for the first step of any doodle: choosing to do it! Of course, you can simply start doodling, too. However, practicing the repeating shapes of the patterns is a great way to coordinate your hand and your mind.

Draw a light sketch using a pencil, or directly ink shapes to start. And remember, it's just as important *how* you make the first marks when you're uncertain as *what* shapes you make. Make your second mark and third mark and so on in response to your first. So begin purposefully, without great concern, and avoid forceful, anxious, or stabbing strokes. You'll relax and be more confident as you proceed. And even when it seems everything is going your way, you still need to maintain balance and pace.

Pen grip.

PLANNING

After you draw the first few shapes, the process will become more fluid. However, you might also find yourself hesitating, unsure of what to do next.

Choosing to create the next mark is an important step you must take in the process. When you're more familiar with the pace, you'll start to imagine multiple directions your doodle can take. These glimpses and your choices are the way you plan a doodle in the moment, from the inside out.

Pencil grip.

DRAWING WITH INK

You can sketch complex tangles with light pencil lines first. Draw the main contours with strokes or dots in ink, and embellish and modify the initial inked lines with thicker parts, filling in crevices for emphasis and to add value.

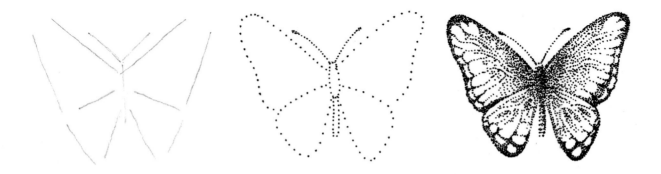

After completing each section, squint and scan your doodle to better see the value pattern. Then go back and increase contrast by filling voids with shading, lines, or dots. Or modify the texture by adding areas of dotted contours or shading, called *stippling*. Color shapes black to intensify the tangle patterning and to add visual punch.

You can add shading to your doodle anytime as you're drawing, but wait until the end to add little touches to adjust the darkest values.

DOODLE ANATOMY

Now that you know how to start a doodle, let's take a closer look at some of the lines, shapes, patterns, and other pieces you can create and combine to build your doodle.

DRAWING UNITS

The *unit* is the smallest element of a doodle. Each unit is made of a line, and sometimes shading that, when repeated, has a strong textural and tonal effect. A unit can be a short, straight line simply turned in regular ways to produce a woven effect. Other common units are the English-language letters *L, S, J,* and *U* and the circle, square, and triangle.

> A *pattern* is made of a repeating *motif,* or a *tangle.* The motif/tangle is made of one or more *units.*

Combine units with lines, shapes, and shading for even greater illusionistic effect. Here are some examples:

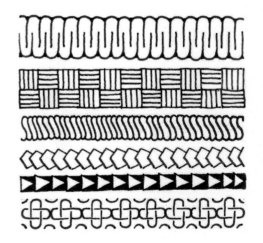

Combine units to create patterns.

CHAPTER 2: DESIGN

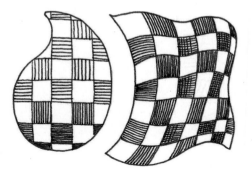

You can modify the same units to produce different illusions.

CREATING SECTIONS

Some motifs or tangles repeat to create a *section*, or an allover field of texture and tone. Others are effective as borders or stripes.

You can crop sections of repeating units and patterns to produce a range of effects. Fill a section with a repeating pattern that appears to stop at the section contour to create a crisp and flat look. Or allow the pattern to distort to fit the section's shape for a 3-D effect.

JOINING SECTIONS

An alternative to making patterns with distinct boundaries is to gradually transition one pattern into another. This has a softer, more dynamic effect. Practice this with tangles that have a balance of similarities and differences. Change the proportions of the interior spaces, draw curves to have more or less tension, and add or reduce shading.

Your skill and personal taste will be evident in the way you combine tangles to create unique effects. With experience and intuition, you can create your own unique tangles. Construct them on a simple dot or line grid by combining parts of existing patterns and basic pattern units. Or create a collection of patterns from this book's reference section or from an internet search. Record them along with your inventions in a sketchbook for reference as you work.

Although each doodler is guided by personal taste to create unique visions, you can make effective statements by wisely weaving together basic units according to the tone each creates. The skillful use of less often says more.

CREATING UNITY

A doodle is a dynamic balance of unity and variety—of similar things and different things. You can achieve perfect doodle harmony with endless repetition of one simple pattern, but that would also yield a boring design.

The skill in creating satisfying harmony comes from balancing it with a necessary amount of variety. When a doodle has unity, all parts fit together seamlessly, making one visual statement.

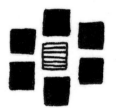

Elements that are close together appear to relate and have unity.

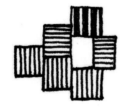

Elements that are similar but with variations and share edges have unity.

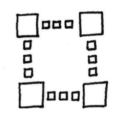

Elements arranged into a shape have unity.

Aligned elements have unity and are seen as one line.

An easy way to create unity is to place all the sections close together so they share borders, like adjacent countries on a map. Strengthen this by choosing similar shapes, colors, sizes, and textures for each section. Enhance this by allowing slight variation when you repeat an element or quality.

WORKING WITH CONTRAST

The amount of difference of dark and light areas in an image is known as *contrast*. Arranging patterns according to contrast plays a key role in improving your Zen doodles. Squint to see the overall tone of a pattern or the arrangement of a doodle's tonal shapes. The general appearance of a doodle's tone without details is its *value pattern*.

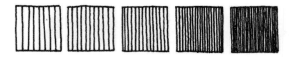 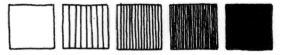

When the tonal range is narrow (left), the contrast is low; the greater the range and difference (right), the greater the contrast.

Many effects within a doodle depend on the contrast of values and the variety of shapes. You can draw repeating shapes to become smaller and paler to create the illusion of depth. Or you can carefully arrange dots, lines, and shapes to achieve continuous tone gradations that rival pencil shading.

Choose a pattern with greater contrast to be a focal point and choose another with less contrast to be a transitional bridge between two patterns. Learn the visual weight and power of the various patterns to skillfully play one off another. As you do, check the value pattern to see how your tangle choices modify it.

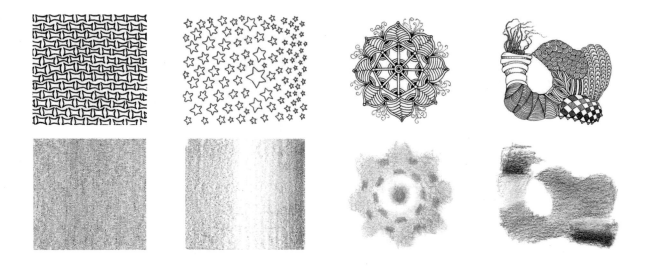

EMPHASIS

You may have noticed that a Zen doodle is made of a lot of parts, or elements. It's fun to repeat the strokes of a motif and to see a pattern develop, but as you progress with your art, you'll want to form your patterns into meaningful shapes that relate to each other with a unified look.

CREATING A FOCAL POINT

You also might want to create an area of main emphasis, or a *focal point*. The focal point has prime importance over all the other parts of the doodle as well as a unique look with greater complexity. Although it draws the most attention, it still appears to be part of the whole. You can create a doodle to have visual impact that builds section by section.

LEVELS OF IMPORTANCE

To better see the abstract qualities of your art, step back and view it from about 20 feet (6m) away as if you're walking into a room and seeing it for the first time. Notice the visual effect. What do you see that attracts your interest? If a work is weak from this distance, it's usually because the value pattern is poor and the main shape is unbalanced.

Now take three steps forward. You should be able to see levels of importance, or *visual hierarchy*, where a more important area is supported by well-balanced but less-important elements. You also should be able to obtain the visual reward of the focal point at 6 feet (1.75m) away from your art, although you'll enjoy the details standing much closer. When elements of a doodle have different importance, it helps you organize the image in your mind. Refine these levels to create a visual path where one section leads to another, and another, and on to the focal point. A simple form of this is evident where sections radiate or twirl around a center point. Another form of visual path parallels the way some cultures read: in a Z-shape path beginning in an upper corner, traveling across the top, then diagonally back to the starting side, then repeated. Not all visual paths are this logical, however. To increase your awareness of this, study all kinds of 2-D images and notice how your eyes travel from part to part. *Continuation,* where one element leads to another, is a powerful unifying force.

VISUAL PATH

1. Your gaze enters the image area.

2. Your eyes are attracted by the striped triangle pointing downward.

3. Your gaze is brought to the secondary emphasis.

4. Again, the stripes attract your eye and direct it upward.

5. Your gaze reaches the main focal point, which is perceived as being most important due to its size, placement, and light value. Its shape also implies movement.

6. You search for finer detail and find it nearby.

7. The frame device guides your gaze upward and directs you to the entry.

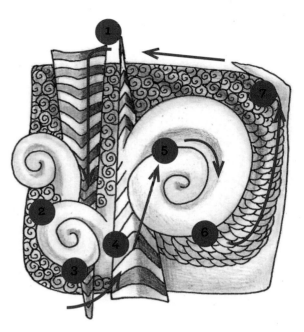

This element of secondary emphasis is a variation of the focal point and is less important because it has smaller spirals.

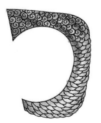

This is the main focal point and the most obvious and memorable point of interest because it's largest and placed prominently.

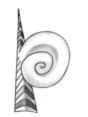

This element has the lowest emphasis and contains the finest detail and a lot of visual interest at close range.

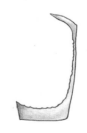

This element is a framing device and provides little visual interest. Through continuation, it guides your gaze upward to the tip of the focal point.

BALANCE

Balance and symmetry are everywhere, from the human bodies to plants and other aspects of the natural world. Because it's so prevalent around us, it's also a criterion for how we perceive and judge artworks.

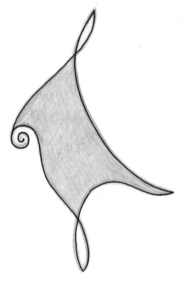

Asymmetrical.

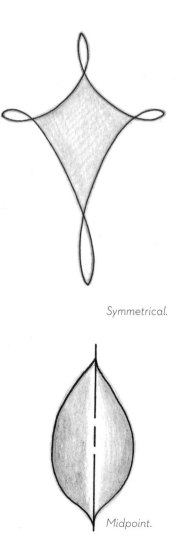

Symmetrical.

Midpoint.

Similar to the body's symmetry, drawn shapes, when analyzed, can have a central axis that runs the length of the shape. When the central axis of a shape divides it into identical, mirror-image halves, the shape is symmetrical. Images, too, are divided in half by a vertical center called a midpoint. When the left side of the image mirrors the right side, it's symmetrical.

CHAPTER 2: DESIGN

You might feel a false shifting of your center of gravity in reaction to observing dynamically positioned shapes.

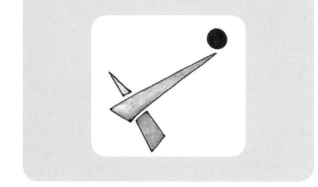

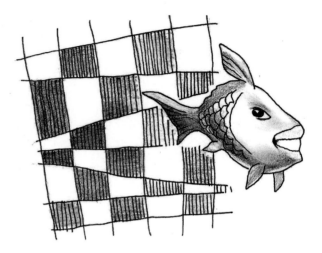

Even with small variations from one side to another, a symmetrical image has a formal or static appearance, like a mandala. Symmetry compels one to contemplate or scrutinize the halves. Mandalas can have a rotational symmetry where the same shape repeats around a center like numbers on the face of a clock.

A shape or area that cannot be divided into equal halves has *asymmetrical* balance. This has a dynamic quality and may appear to lean or imply movement.

Shifts in balance do not always occur across the image's midpoint or only between two things. Doodles are made of many interwoven shapes and values and often have a convoluted balance you follow intuitively. Sometimes it's a mystery how the maze of shapes and patterns of a Zen doodle balances and draws you inward.

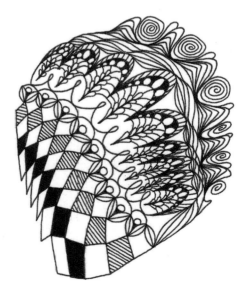

3

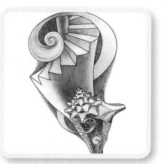

CREATIVITY

Reason and imagination are the two hemispheres of a creative mind. One side sees a broken shell, while the other considers the sand-polished, ivory-colored, broken-cased, ridged, patterned spiral inside and wonders, *What if* ...

GETTING IDEAS

Ideas for doodles are everywhere, although you might need to learn to look differently at what's around you to find inspiration. For example, what if a shell was combined with a stairway? The spiral staircase implies there was such a realization. Combining unlike things is a small part of the idea-generating process, or *ideation*. It's a stage in creation during which you can consider possibilities. Random combinations can produce curiously attractive blends. Try it for yourself, and fill your sketchbook with the following visual challenges:

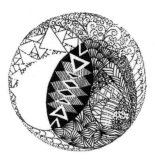

1. Draw possible tangle combinations that work well within a circular doodle main shape.

2. Draw 10 possible doodle main shapes with section divisions in 10 minutes.

3. Research Zen doodles online and list 10 new doodle structures you would like to try creating.

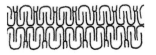 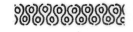

4. Combine capital letter Cs in various ways to create shapes and patterns where it's not easy to see you're designing with Cs. Try this with four more letters, too.

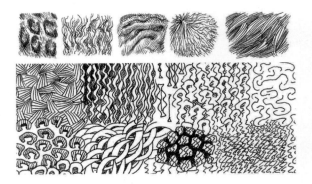

5. Research and draw animal fur textures, and use these to create new patterns.

6. List 50 adjectives that are visual qualities a doodle pattern can have.

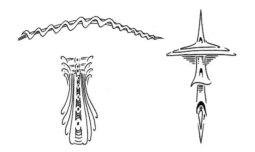

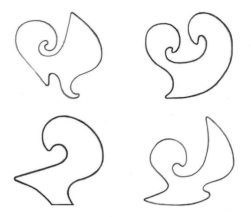

7. Go to a park, listen to the sounds you hear, and draw visual equivalents for the sounds. Have others guess what sounds your doodles illustrate.

9. Draw four irregular shapes with the same dimensions. Give each shape curved and straight contours that, when viewed as a group, have a balance of unity and variety.

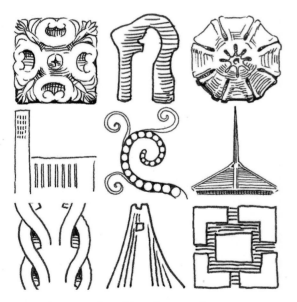

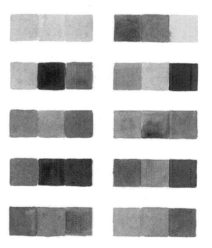

8. In your sketchbook, copy linear patterns found on architecture, jewelry, ornaments, furniture, and textiles.

10. Create a collection of 40 different colored squares made from paint swatches. Randomly pick three and color them in squares in your sketchbook using colored pencils or markers. Repeat this to make 10 different color sets. Produce a doodle colored with three colors from one of the sets.

FINDING IDEAS IN NATURE

Plants and creatures are a rich source for visual ideas. Begin by choosing a simple natural object. Draw its main, outer shape first. Then add cross-contour lines and some shading. Next, draw a shape you see in the form that may be partially or totally visible in the first drawing of the object. Draw as many of these isolated shapes as you find in the object. Repeat this with nine other natural forms. Finally, create 10 doodle patterns using these natural shapes.

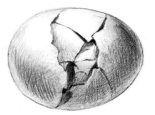

1. Choose a natural object (in this case, a cracked eggshell).

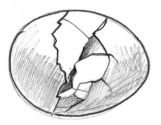

2. Draw the object's contour. Then add cross-contour lines and shading.

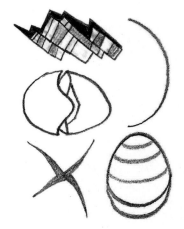

3. Isolate and exaggerate the shapes you see in the form.

CHAPTER 3: CREATIVITY

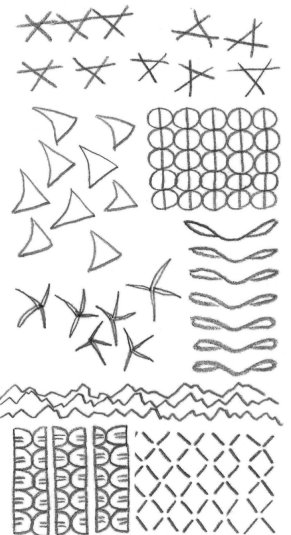

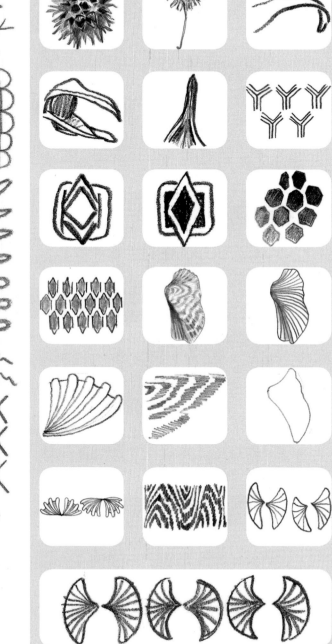

4. Create doodle patterns based on the shapes from step 3.

TURNING IDEAS INTO DOODLES

Once you develop some ideas, inspired by nature or otherwise, it's time to put them together into a full, larger doodle. Be sure you first create at least 10 patterns from which to choose.

You can turn ideas into doodles in several ways:

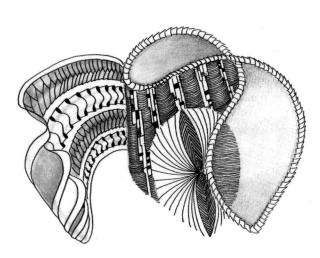

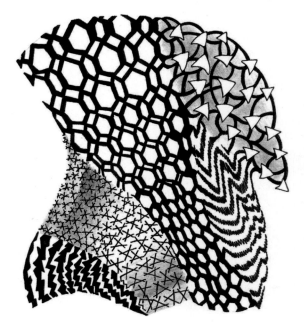

You could draw an irregular main shape first and add divisions to create sections to fill in.

Or you can combine a few patterns to make another doodle with a different irregular shape.

CHAPTER 3: CREATIVITY

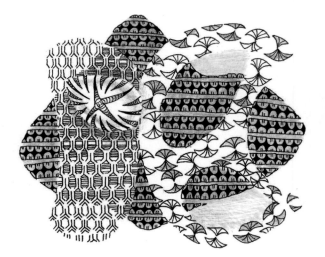

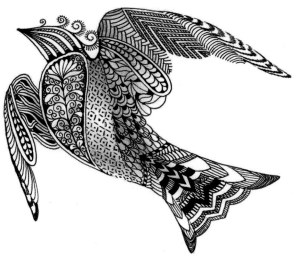

You don't have to isolate the patterns. You can combine and overlap them in groups.

You also can choose a few patterns and fill them into a silhouette of an animal. First, draw the contour of the animal shape and then divide it with curving lines to make sections. To create a subtle 3-D illusion, you can shade the completed doodle.

Write in your sketchbook or consider: when you look at your doodles, is there one that stands out as being more visually satisfying? Why? How do value pattern, visual hierarchy, and continuation play a role in the success of a doodle? What other factors affect their unity when viewed as a group?

COMBINING TWO PATTERNS

Some of the fun of doodling comes from inventing. By modifying existing patterns and combining various parts to make new patterns, you increase your motif and tangle library.

While you practice doodling, collect your motifs and copy them into your sketchbook. As you do, notice the strokes and small units of each. These are the building blocks you can use to form new motifs and patterns. Write your personal observations beside the drawings and possibly where and when you found them. Then, build your doodling resources by creating a new motif from two you already have. Here's how:

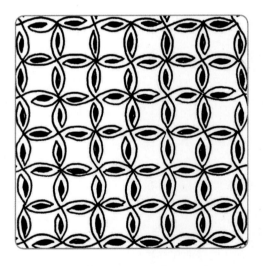

1. Draw three ³⁄₄-inch (2cm) square grids lined up side by side with a little space between them. Draw an existing pattern in the left grid and another in the right one. Then take a strong element from the left one and draw it in the grid in the middle. Do the same for the right side. Fill in the rest of the center motif area with other elements chosen from the outer two patterns, and transition the parts to connect.

2. Redraw the new motif on a clean section of the page. Look for its potential for pattern by repeating it in a block of nine squares, grouped in an organic shape or, if appropriate, repeating in a band.

CHAPTER 3: CREATIVITY

Now try this with other motifs and tangles. As you invent, think of combinations that are easy to draw and that have effective value patterns.

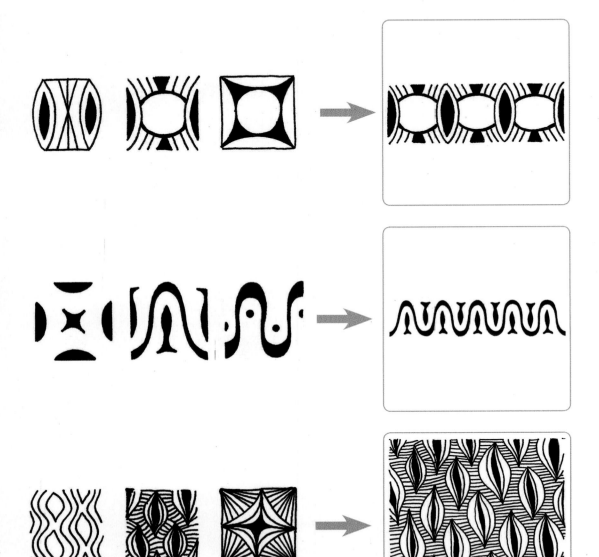

4

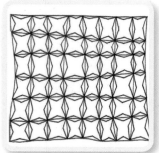

GRIDS

Patterns of repeating motifs can often be organized neatly on a *grid,* a structure of intersecting vertical and horizontal lines. Especially when creating complex visual textures, drawing a grid in pencil first frees you to concentrate more on the quality of the inked lines and less on their orientation and how far apart to make them. Geometric patterns can be constructed on a penciled grid easily, but you also can align and more accurately place any repeating element with this handy device. As with most construction lines, lightly drawn grids appear to fade and disappear when much darker inked lines are laid over them.

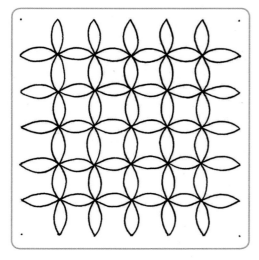

CREATING A DOTTED GRID

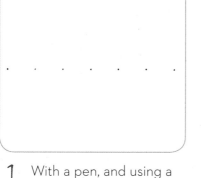

You can build many rich geometric patterns with curves and diagonals on a field of evenly spaced dots. The illusion of overlapping circles in this pattern results from simply repeating the leaf motif vertically and horizontally.

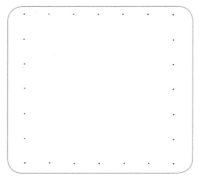

1 With a pen, and using a ruler as a guide, create a row of seven dots spaced ½ inch (1.25cm) apart.

2 Rotate your paper 90 degrees and make six dots aligned with the last dot of the previous row to create a frame of evenly spaced dots.

3 Fill the frame with evenly spaced dots that align with the frame dots. Use the previous row as a guide.

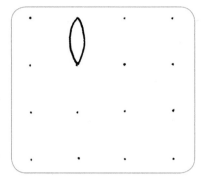

4   Starting at the second dot in the top row, draw two lines curving down to the dot directly below.

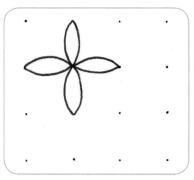

5   Create similar petal forms with curved lines stretching outward from the center dot.

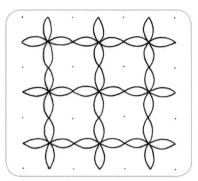

6   Fill the area with a four-petal flower tangle so the tips of the petals touch.

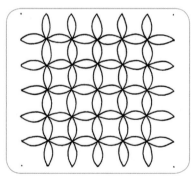

7   Draw more of the four-petal tangle to fill the interior areas.

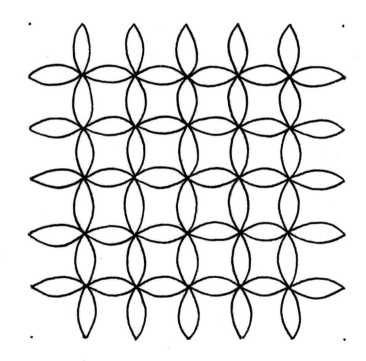

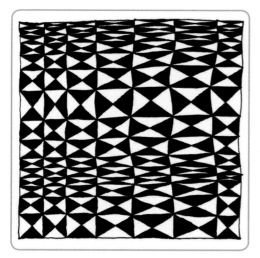

CREATING DISTORTION WITH A GRID

You can alternate the distance between vertical and horizontal grid lines to distort a pattern that will appear to undulate like fabric and soften the hard geometric effect. Begin the grid with wavy lines to further intensify the effect.

> The distance between the last few verticals can be shorter if necessary to fit the original L width.

1 With a .05mm ink pen, draw an L shape with two hand-drawn lines 3½ inches (9cm) long.

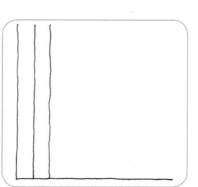

2 Draw two somewhat wavy vertical grid lines parallel to the first and approximately ½ inch (1.25cm) apart.

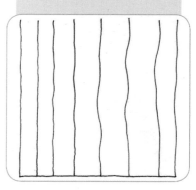

3 Draw more wavy vertical lines increasingly farther apart.

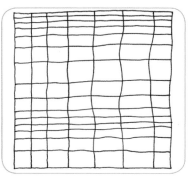

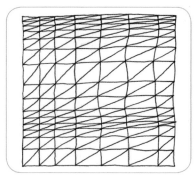

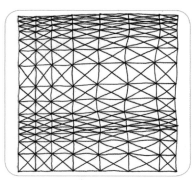

4 Draw wavy horizontal grid lines that gradually become closer and then farther apart.

5 Make a diagonal line from the lower-left corner to the upper-right corner in every grid box.

6 Draw another diagonal in each grid box that crosses the one you drew in step 5.

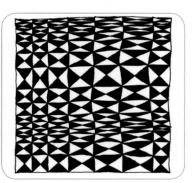

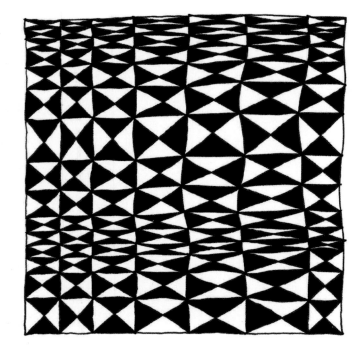

7 Box by box, fill in opposing triangles with black ink to create a bowtie tangle pattern.

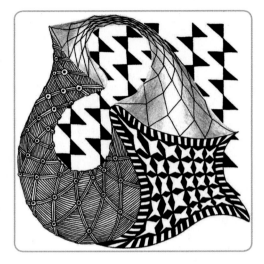

CREATING A DOODLE WITH A GRID

Grids made of curving lines support the illusion of 3-D, while grids with straight lines appear flat. The illusion of depth is further enhanced in this doodle by using overlapping and contrasting patterns.

1 With a pencil, draw the curvy main shape of the doodle.

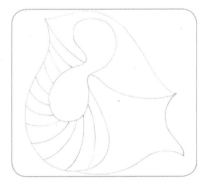

2 Draw curving cross-contour lines in the left section.

3 Lay in more curving lines that cross the previous ones diagonally.

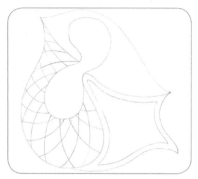

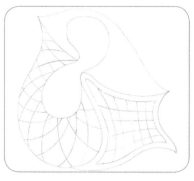

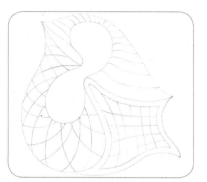

4 In the lower-right section, pencil in a contour parallel to the section contour.

5 Add curving vertical and horizontal lines in this section to create a distorted grid.

6 Draw curving cross-contour lines in the upper section.

After drawing their contours, mark the triangles to be inked with pencil shading.

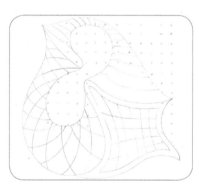

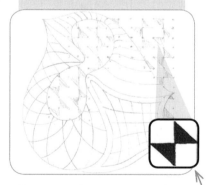

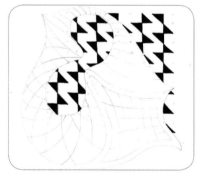

7 With your pencil at a 30-degree angle to the paper, lightly create a dotted grid background.

8 Draw the contours of the **bow tie** tangle by connecting dots of the background grid.

9 Using black ink, color in the bow ties.

Not sure how to draw a tangle? This icon indicates creating the doodle is explained elsewhere in the book.

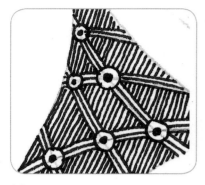

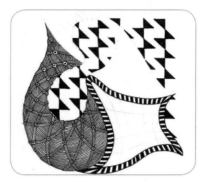

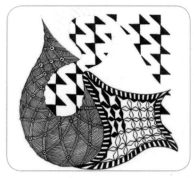

10 Ink circles and dots at the intersections of the left shape, and draw lines connecting them. Then shade the tangle interiors with parallel lines.

11 Create an alternating pattern by inking cross-contour stripes in the contour band area of the lower-right section.

12 Using the grid in the lower-right shape, repeat the V shape, and color the resulting diamond shapes.

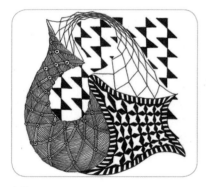

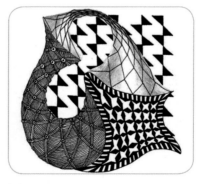

13 Draw zigzags across the bands of the upper section that alternate every other band so their points touch.

14 Shade the upper section with a pencil so it's darker along the outside edges.

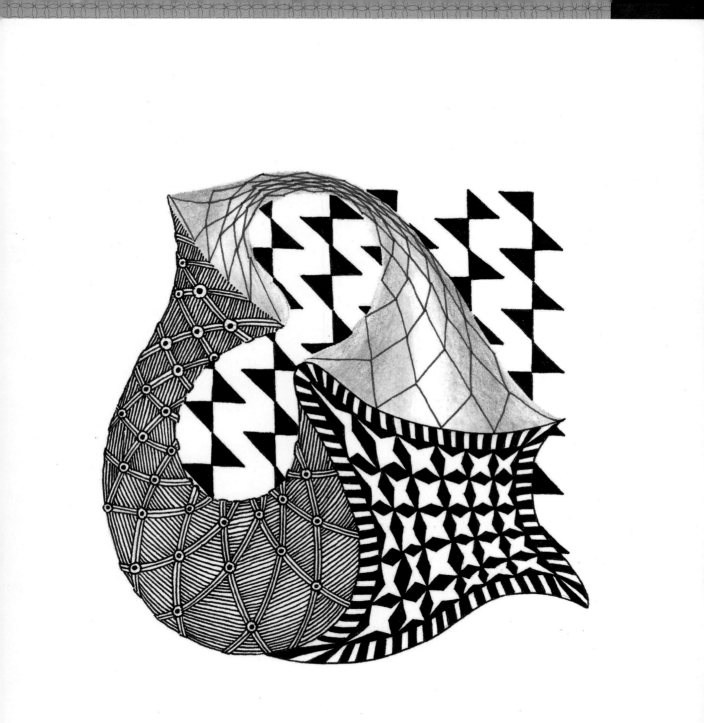

CREATING A DOODLE WITH A GRID

5

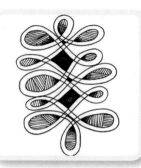

KNOTS AND BRAIDS

Countless artisans and artists, from China to Ireland, have found inspiration in knot and braid forms. Get started doodling knot basics like overlapping and alternating rhythm, and you'll see that these forms are a rich and very expressive resource.

Knots and braids are built on motifs that repeat in a row, column, or around a center point as many times as needed to fill a space. The individual character of a pattern is in the motif, as you'll notice when you look at the natural sources they imitate. Inspect braided hair and diagrams of sailors' knots, for example, or study how some patterns incorporate cultural icons like hearts and crosses or geometric shapes. You'll discover many subtle designs simply by replicating patterns from images of stone carvings and ancient calligraphy and embellishing them with your own creativity.

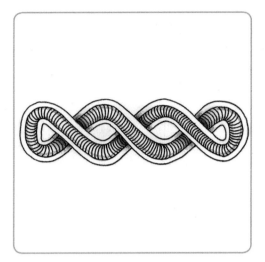

OVERLAP AND SHADING

The elegance of a braid or knot is enhanced with a surface treatment. Ink a repeating motif on the surface and then shade with a pencil with short, back-and-forth strokes to add light and shadow effects.

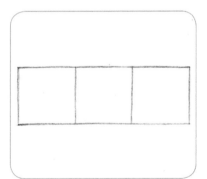

1 Draw three squares connected in a row, creating a divided, long rectangle.

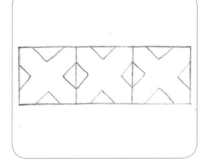

2 Draw triangles centered on each side of the squares.

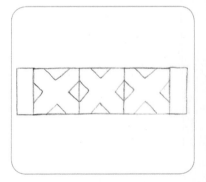

3 Draw vertical rectangles onto the ends of the long rectangle.

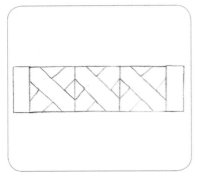

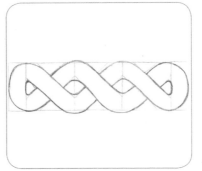

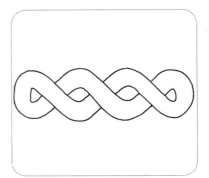

4 In each square, connect the tips of the top and right triangles and the left and bottom triangles with diagonal lines.

5 Lighten the sketch from step 4 with an eraser, and using the light lines as a guide, refine the form to be rounded.

6 Lighten the sketch again, and ink the final contours.

After shading, soften the effect by rubbing the surface with a fine-tipped blending stump.

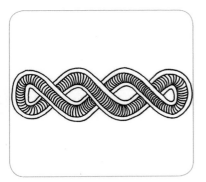

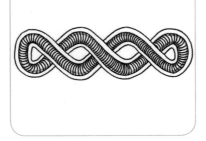

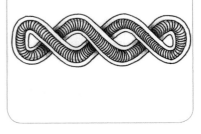

7 Draw contours parallel to the edge, and fill the center space with repeating curved lines.

8 Shade the edges of the interior section.

9 Shade where the upper part of the form overlaps the lower part.

OVERLAP AND SHADING

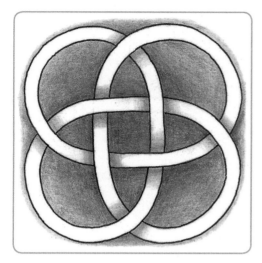

CELTIC KNOT

You can use a midpoint grid to create many intricate knot forms with rotational symmetry. However complex a version of the knot is, the strand always passes over and under in an alternating pattern.

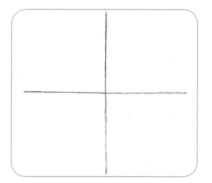

1 Sketch a grid with vertical and horizontal guidelines 3 inches (7.5cm) long that cross at their centers.

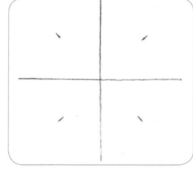

2 On an imaginary diagonal halfway between the ends of each pair of grid axes, make a small mark.

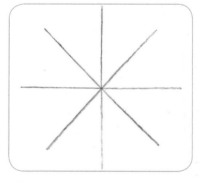

3 Connect the pairs of marks to form an X.

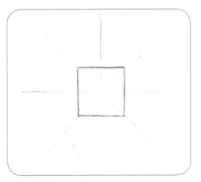

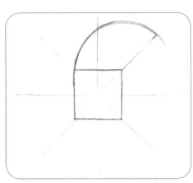

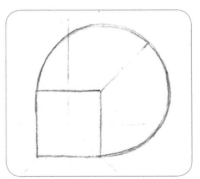

4   Draw a small square centered on the grid guidelines. Lighten the guidelines created in steps 1 and 3 if necessary.

5   Draw a line that curves from the square's upper-left corner to the upper-right end of the diagonal axis.

6   Continue the curve from step 5 to the square's lower-right corner.

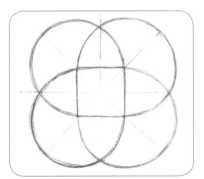

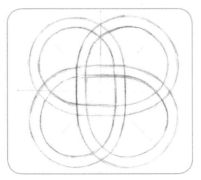

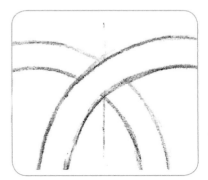

7   Repeat the curved form in the other three grid quadrants.

8   Sketch a line inside and parallel to the knot contour.

9   At the top of the knot, erase two small interior lines so the right part appears to pass over the left.

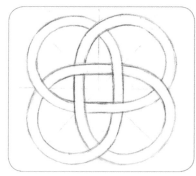 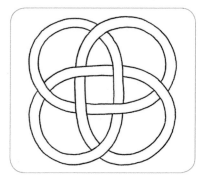 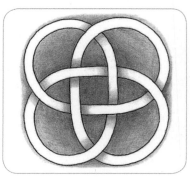

10 Throughout the form, erase lines at each juncture to alternate the direction of the overlap illusion.

11 Ink the contour lines. When dry, erase any visible pencil lines.

12 Shade with an HB pencil using the side of the tip at the overlapping parts and around the form.

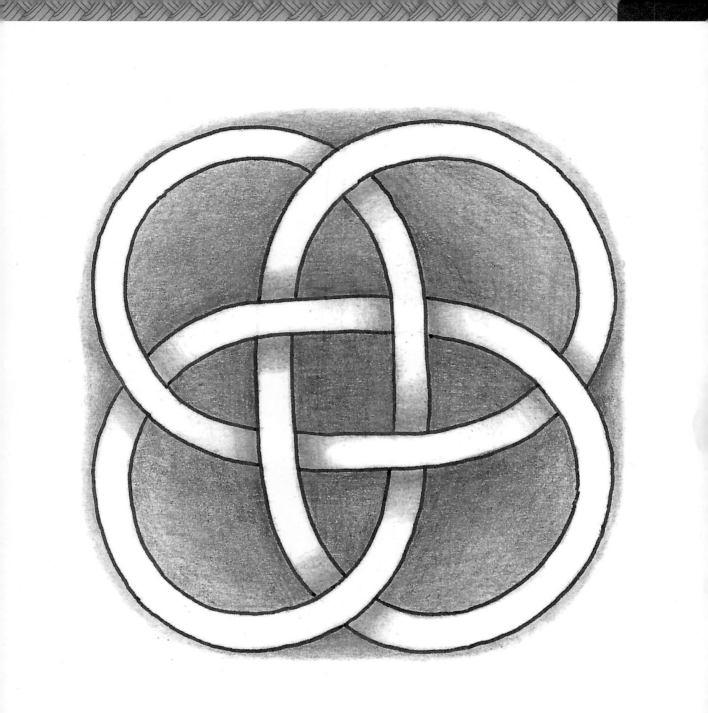

CELTIC KNOT

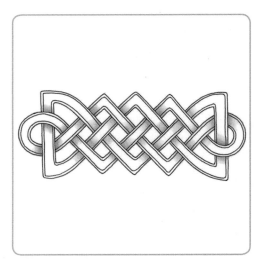

LONG CELTIC KNOT

Designs like this can be found carved into ancient stones across Ireland and Britain. Use them in doodles to fill rectangular areas, as a graphic frame, or for unusual texture with visual weight.

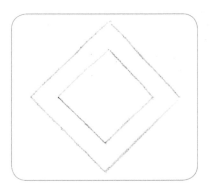

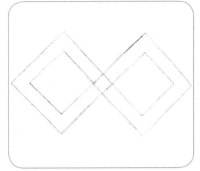

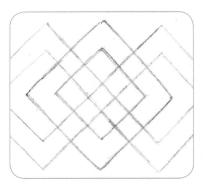

1 Sketch a diamond shape about 2 inches (5cm) tall. Then draw a diamond centered inside about 1⅛ inches (2.75cm) tall.

2 Repeat step 1 to the right of the original diamond, and overlap the corners.

3 Draw another double diamond centered between the diamonds from steps 1 and 2.

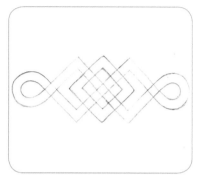

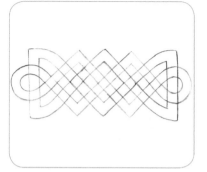

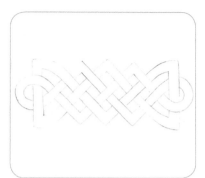

4 Add teardrop shapes overlapping the outside corners of the left and right diamond corners.

5 Draw rounded triangular shapes that overlap the outside corners of the inside double diamond.

6 Erase extra lines in the overlapping areas, alternating over and under throughout the form.

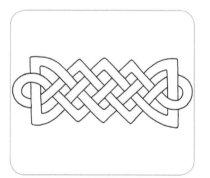

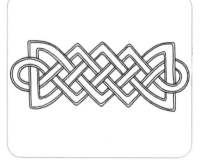

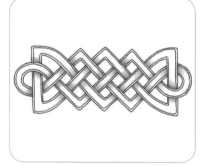

7 Ink the entire form's contours, rotating your paper as you draw the contours to avoid smudging the lines.

8 Add interior contours parallel to both edges of the form.

9 Shade the form with a pencil where it passes under the bridging sections.

LONG CELTIC KNOT

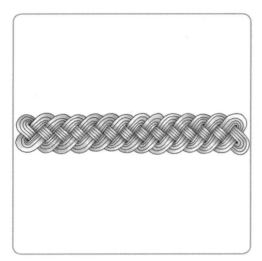

BRAID

This braid is based on ancient Celtic patterns carved into stone, but its pattern mimics hair when shaded. Objects with a strong blend of 2-D and 3-D illusion can have great graphic appeal.

It's easier to judge that the box shape is balanced if you draw it as a level square.

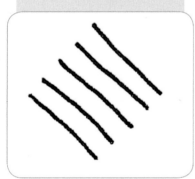

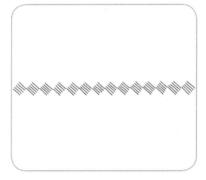

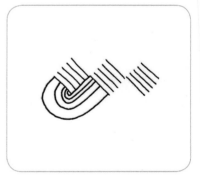

1 Rotate your paper 45 degrees to the right, and draw five short strokes grouped in a box shape.

2 Make a column of the box shapes and then rotate your paper left, back to the straight, starting position.

3 Draw five lines that curve from the side of the second box to the side of the leftmost one.

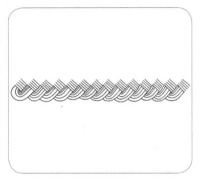

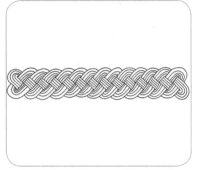

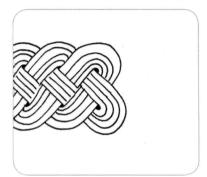

4 Draw curves from the previous curve group to the underside of each box.

5 Draw curves along the top of the form as in step 4.

6 Color in the small interior gaps where the form curves.

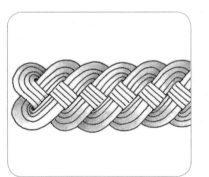

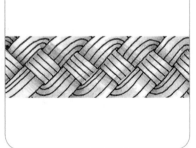

7 Using a pencil, shade a shadow where the form is overlapped.

8 Shade the sides of the central weave sections, leaving a highlight in the center of the box shape.

6

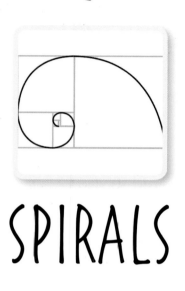

SPIRALS

Curling forms have always been significant to world cultures, interpreted as symbols of the sun, fertility, change, rebirth, and life itself. And after all the interpretations, the spiral is still an inspiration to artists.

You can group spirals to create the look of dense ground cover or delicate filigree by tightening or loosening the rotations. Spirals help teach the importance of staying in the present and focusing only on the thing you're drawing. Thinking about filling sections with hundreds of spirals can make drawing them seem tedious. However, you can find the joy of spirals by allowing each one to be unique. Then you'll see that they're fun to make.

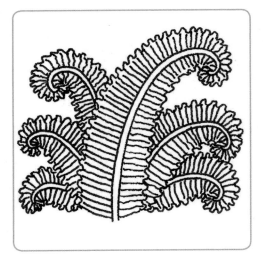

FERN

Many plants unfurl from a tight spiral. These fern fronds contrast a curling white center with a pleated surface and a wavy edge. You can adapt this doodle into borders, allover patterns, and organic themes.

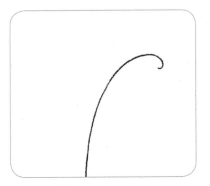

1 Begin with the long curve of the midrib of the nearest fern frond.

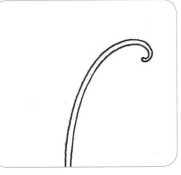

2 Complete the midrib by adding the other side and the tip.

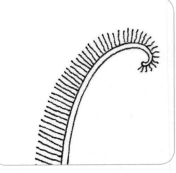

3 Draw slightly wavy lines perpendicular to the curving midrib that become shorter toward the tip.

CHAPTER 6: SPIRALS

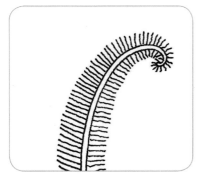

4 Add the other side of short lines.

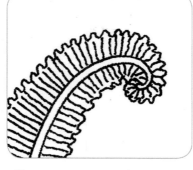

5 Draw an irregular wavy line to create the frond's exterior texture.

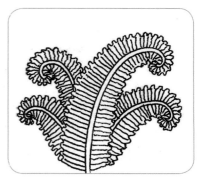

6 Draw more fronds that curve left and right from the upper part of the first frond.

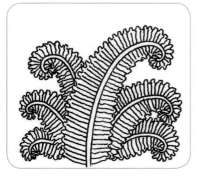

7 Complete this tangle by adding two lower fronds.

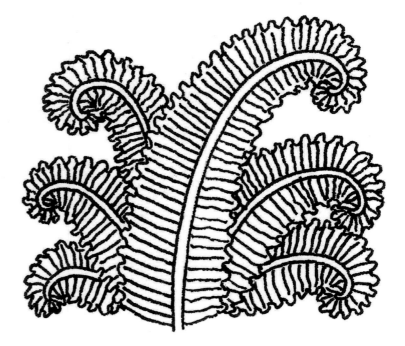

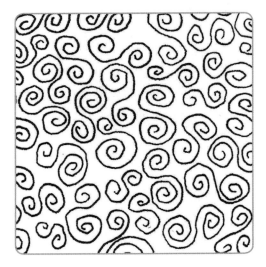

SASSY

This tangle is made by repeating two linked and relaxed spirals and by changing the direction of each S shape. To help liberate this tangle to be truly sassy, try drawing it with your nondominant hand.

1 Begin by spiraling out from the center for two or three rotations. Then, without lifting your pen, draw another spiral curling inward.

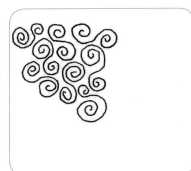

2 Rotate your paper, and draw another tangle unit. Repeat, changing the size of your spirals.

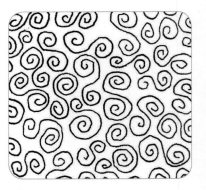

3 Fill the entire section with sassy spirals, stopping to squint at your work occasionally to ensure the overall tone is even.

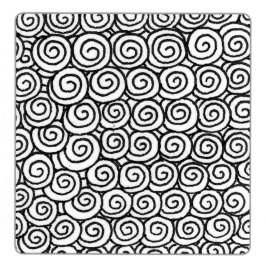

TWIRL

This fun tangle is a small, closed spiral repeated with slight variations. Its charm comes from the subtle overlapping of the hypnotic form, producing slight value changes and a dense pattern with great covering power.

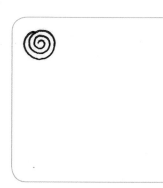

1 Starting in the center, draw a spiral with three revolutions, and close.

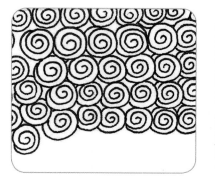

2 Continue creating twirls, underlapping adjacent twirls and allowing for some variation in the arrangement for a more spontaneous look.

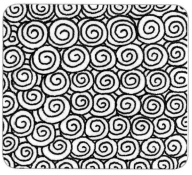

3 In the gaps between the twirls, add curves to balance the overall value and texture.

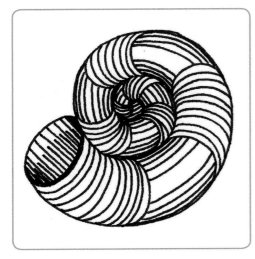

TUBA

This tangle uses cross-contour lines to emphasize the tubelike quality of the snail shell form. Lateral cross-contour lines draw attention to side-to-side roundness, while longitudinal ones flow the length of the form to its center.

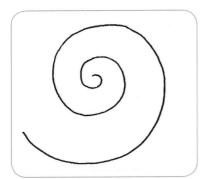

1 Beginning at the center, slowly draw a spiral that widens in three clockwise rotations.

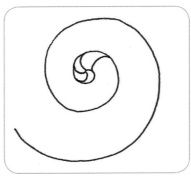

2 Add cross-contour curves that become farther apart as they proceed to the tube's opening.

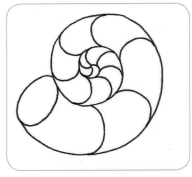

3 Complete the tube's opening with a curve.

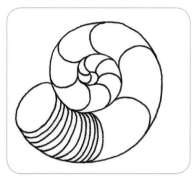

4 Fill in alternating sections of the tube with curving lines that span the form.

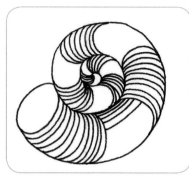

5 Fill in the other sections of the tube with lines that follow the form.

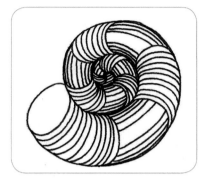

6 Draw longitudinal lines closer together at the outside of the tube form to indicate a curved edge.

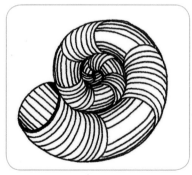

7 Draw lines at the opening, and darken the contour.

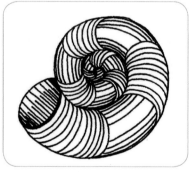

8 Add shading lines between the lines of step 7, and darken the interior contour.

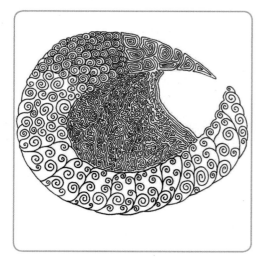

CURLED

This doodle starts with just a few curved lines and ends up resembling a curled leaf shape. The tangles transition gradually from light to dark.

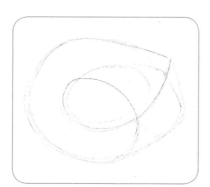

1 Using a pencil, lightly sketch the egg-shape contour of the doodle.

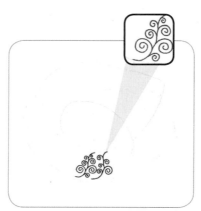

2 Draw a **spiraling** tendril to curve left at the bottom and right at the top.

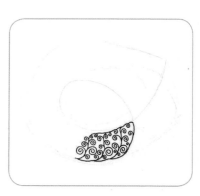

3 Link the individual tendril parts with curves.

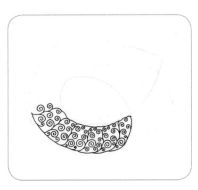

4 Continue the tendrils in the other direction.

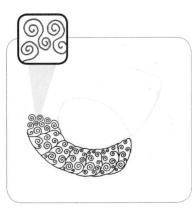

5 Transition into a **S-curl** tangle.

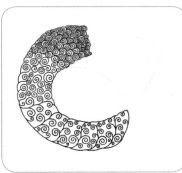

6 Link the contours with more curved lines.

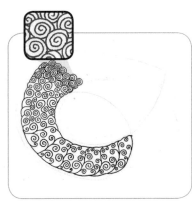

7 Incorporate a **spiral** tangle.

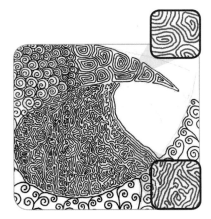

8 Begin to pack the spirals tighter. This intensifies the gradual darkening of the overall value.

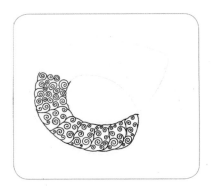

9 Finish the pointed area with a **tortoise shell** motif, and fill the center with a **meander** pattern. Complete the meander section to curve upward. Erase the pencil lines.

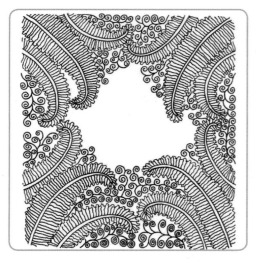

FROND FOREST

Create the visual texture of a lush forest floor by repeating and modifying two tangles: tendril and fern. This doodle balances a frame of dense texture with a much smaller patch of white space.

1 Using a pencil, draw a light rectangle about 4 inches wide by 4 1/2 inches tall (10.5 by 11.5cm).

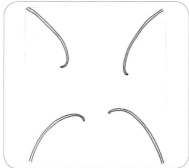

2 Establish the corners of the frame with a frond midrib curving in from each corner.

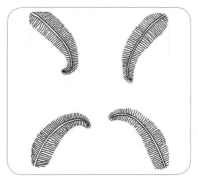

3 Draw the short lines of the fern leaves that radiate from the midribs.

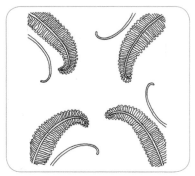

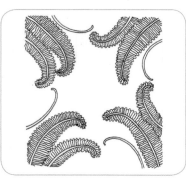

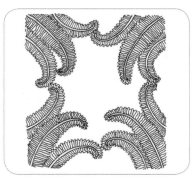

4   Add the wavy contour around the fronds, and draw more midribs for the next fronds close to the others but not touching.

5   Draw the short lines of the leaves and the wavy contour, but don't overlap the corner fronds. Add the next set of midribs.

6   Continue drawing more fronds, allowing them to touch with repeating curves to create interesting enclosed spaces.

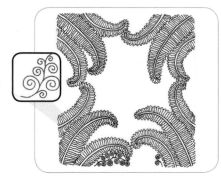

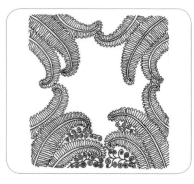

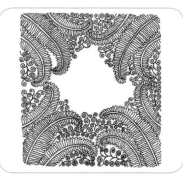

7   Begin a **tendril** motif in the enclosed shapes.

8   Continue drawing tendrils, working from the corners to the middle.

9   Keep building onto the tendrils to create an asymmetrical open area. Erase the pencil lines.

FROND FOREST

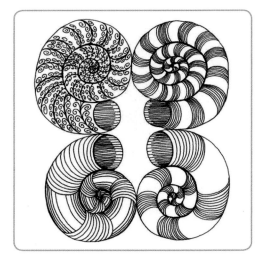

QUARTET

Bilateral symmetry reflects a mirror image of an element across an axis, creating formal balance. Here, the symmetry of the tube forms emphasizes the different pattern of each tube in this eccentric quartet.

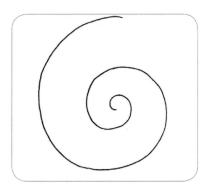

1   In an area about 4 inches wide by 5 inches tall (10 by 12.5cm), draw a spiral in the lower-left quarter.

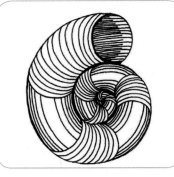

2   Complete the surface detail of the **tuba** tangle.

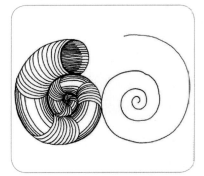

3   Draw another spiral about the same size as the first that reflects it.

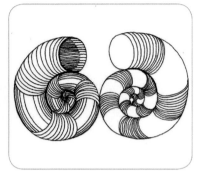

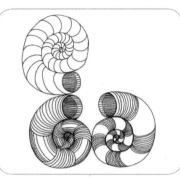

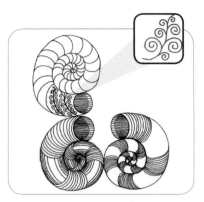

4 Draw cross-contour lines as in the tuba tangle, but leave the alternating sections blank.

5 Above the first tube, draw a tube with cross contours that reflects the tube beneath it. Shade the opening of the new tube with lines as in the previous tubes.

6 Along the cross-contour lines, draw spirals to create a variation of the **tendril** tangle.

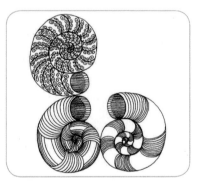

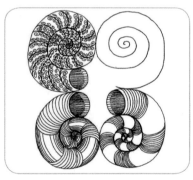

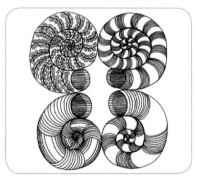

7 Compress the width of the tendrils as you continue to create the illusion of rounding.

8 Next to the third tube, begin a fourth that reflects the others.

9 Alternate curving cross-contours and gaps like the second tube, but at a faster rate. Shade the interior.

7

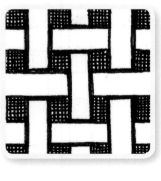

WEAVES

From baskets to burlap, woven forms hold a wealth of inspiration for making Zen doodles. Overlapped strands produce unique shadow patterns you can copy in a logical way by repeating a few shapes on a grid. Raking light on coarse material reveals the characteristic shapes that tell us if a fabric is knitted wool or not.

In fact, when studying any texture for doodling ideas, look past the tiniest details to see the larger shapes and their relationships to one another. Copy them into your sketchbook as accurately as possible, but know that even when you can't quite replicate a form, drawing from life can help you see more clearly actual shapes that can't be imagined.

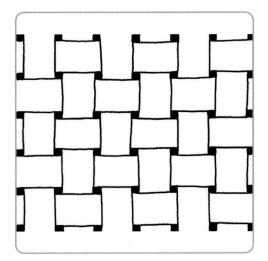

SIMPLE WEAVE

You can alter this basic weave motif easily to create a range of different weave styles. Change the shaded square size, curve the connecting lines, shade beside the overlaps, or even distort the grid to emphasize different qualities.

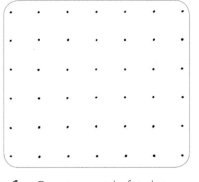

1 Create a grid of 6 dots by 7 dots, each ½ inch (1.25cm) apart.

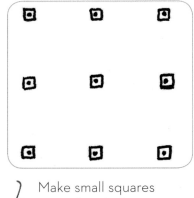

2 Make small squares around each dot.

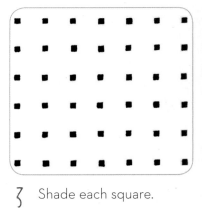

3 Shade each square.

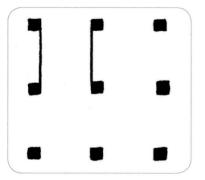

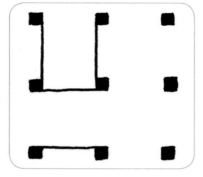

Alternate the pairs of connecting lines to begin the weave pattern.

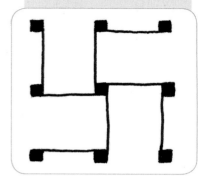

4 In the upper-left group of four squares, connect each side pair of squares with a vertical line on the inside edge.

5 Below the first group of squares, connect the adjoining group of four with horizontal lines on the inside edge.

6 Complete the next two adjoining groups of squares with lines in the opposite directions of the first ones.

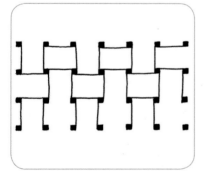

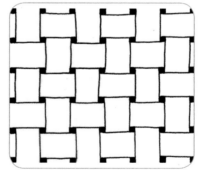

7 Continue connecting the adjoining groups of squares, completing all the verticals in a row first and then the horizontals.

8 Complete the weave by adding the remaining lines.

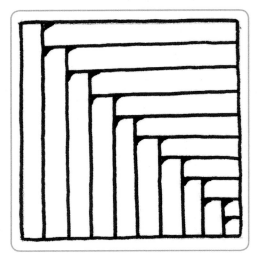

STEPPED WEAVE

This symmetrical pattern is most effective where it can show off its overlapping and shaded corners. Not all doodle patterns look like actual materials, but this one is reminiscent of wicker.

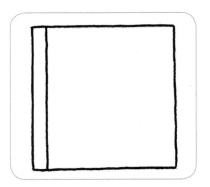

1 Draw a box, and add a vertical line at the left to create a thin vertical rectangle.

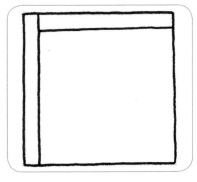

2 Draw a horizontal line at the top that creates a similar rectangular shape as the vertical space at the left.

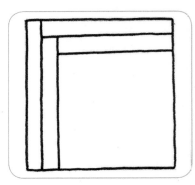

3 Draw another set of vertical and then horizontal divisions.

CHAPTER 7: WEAVES

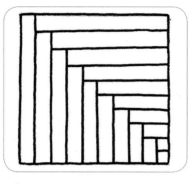

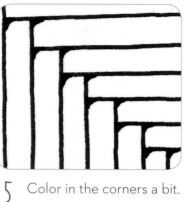

4 Continue the pattern of divisions to the lower right.

5 Color in the corners a bit.

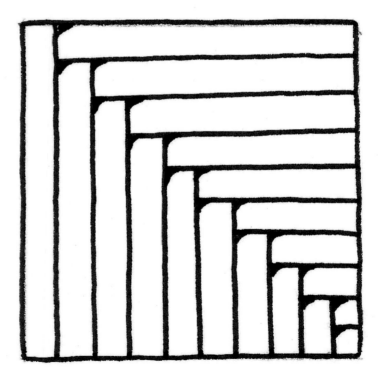

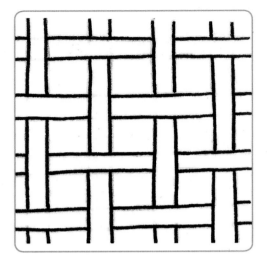

WEAVE OF STRANDS

This weave fills asymmetrical areas well. Simply adjust the strand width and the distance between strands to fill larger or smaller spaces. Leave the gaps irregular for a casual appearance, or color them to emphasize the pattern.

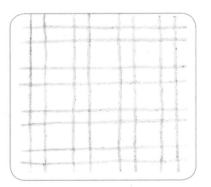

1 Using a pencil, lightly draw narrow pairs of vertical and horizontal lines.

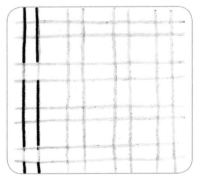

2 Ink the sides of the left vertical strand except for every other horizontal strand.

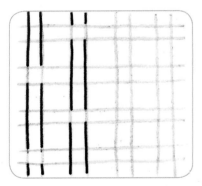

3 Ink the side of the next vertical strand, this time skipping the two horizontal strands you skipped in step 2.

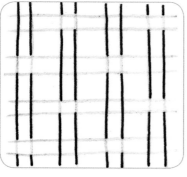 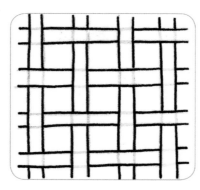 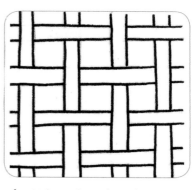

4 Complete the other two vertical strands, and continue the alternating pattern.

5 Draw the sides of the horizontal strands.

6 When the ink is dry, erase any visible pencil lines.

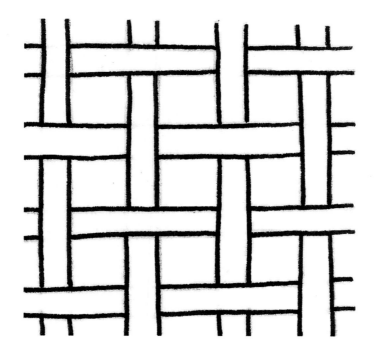

WEAVE OF STRANDS

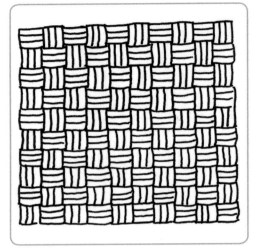

BOX WEAVE

୧ଡ଼ିଡ଼୨

This simple motif of four lines is effective for filling transition sections. The first line in each group is the most critical; be sure it fits with the previous group of lines to create a better 3-D illusion.

1 Draw the motif of four slightly curving lines stacked horizontally.

2 Make a slightly curving vertical line that touches the right side of the previous four lines and then make three more beside it.

3 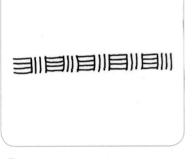 Continue making alternating groups of the motif in a row.

CHAPTER 7: WEAVES

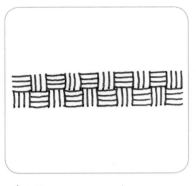

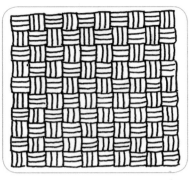

4 Draw a second row so the motifs alternate vertically and horizontally.

5 Add more rows to create a stronger effect. Draw a line on the outside of each open motif to finish the doodle.

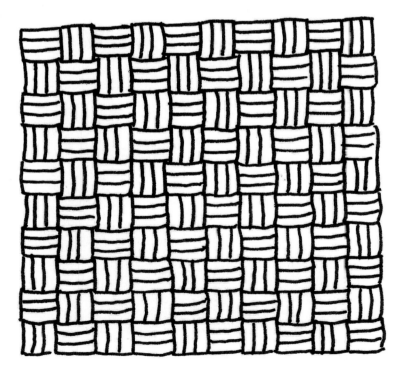

BOX WEAVE

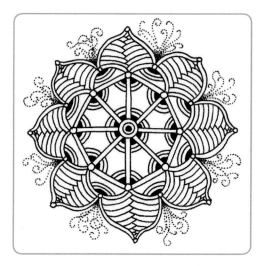

DOODLE WITH A WEAVE

The woven elements of this lotus flower form a transition from the bold center structure to the fine curling texture at the outside edges. The dot-and-connectors method employed here is useful for constructing geometric forms.

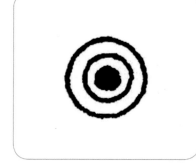

1 Draw a round dot, and draw two circles round it.

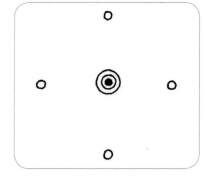

2 Draw four small circles aligned vertically and horizontally with the center dot ½ inch (1.25cm) out from center.

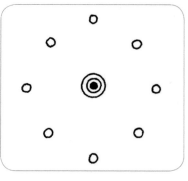

3 Add a small circle between the previous four circles so they all form a ring around the center.

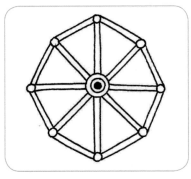

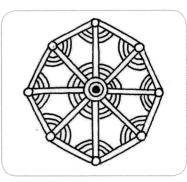

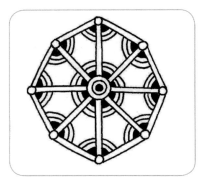

4 Join the circles and the center with pairs of parallel lines.

5 Draw concentric curves in the corners of the triangular spaces.

6 Color the innermost space created by the concentric curves black.

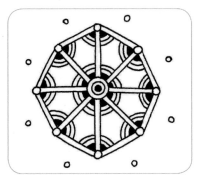

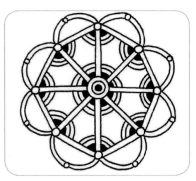

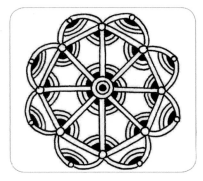

7 Draw a very small circle centered outside the base of each triangular shape.

8 Connect the small dots to the dots at the base of the triangular shapes with pairs of curved lines.

9 Draw concentric curves at the tops of the semicircular shapes, and color the innermost areas black.

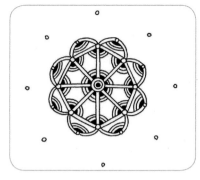

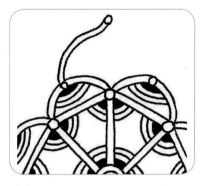

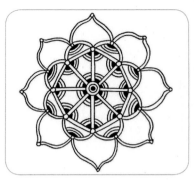

10 Draw small circles about ½ inch (1.25cm) out from the circles created in step 7.

11 Connect the top small circle to the very small dot at the center of the semicircle on the left with a pair of curved lines.

12 Add pairs of curved lines to both the left and right very small dots to create lotus petal shapes.

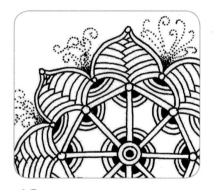

13 Add the weave tangle inside the lotus petals, and draw dotted curves, shading where the petals join.

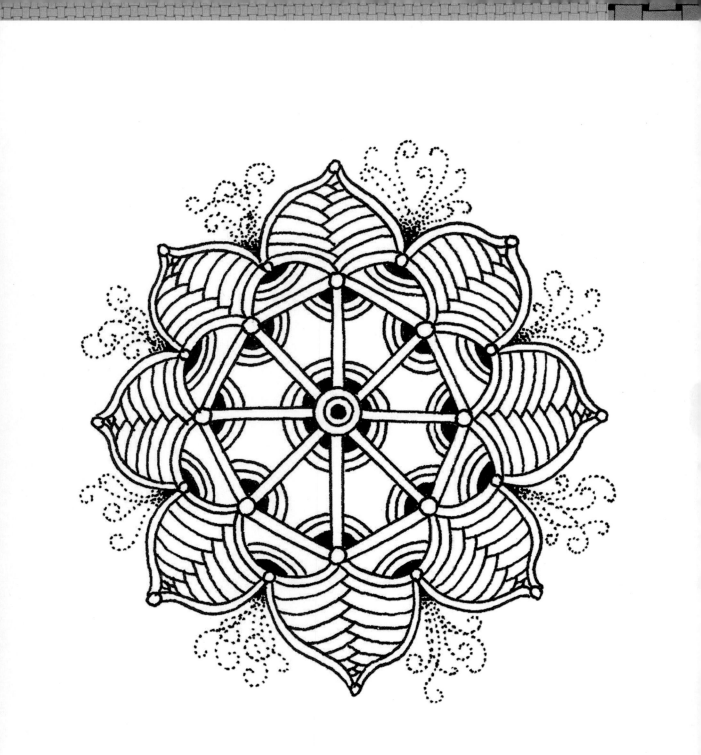

DOODLE WITH A WEAVE

8

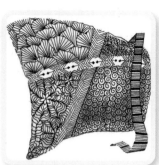

BANDS AND STRIPES

In decorative terms, bands and stripes are lines that span a surface to emphasize 2-D or 3-D qualities. Use them in doodles where you want a formal look or to add stability.

Stripes are often grouped in a colorful dark/light pattern, while a band is more ornate and appears to bind something together. Vertical bands or stripes can emphasize height, horizontal elements draw attention to width, and diagonals suggest movement.

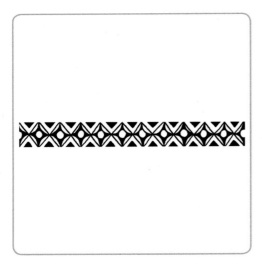

EVEN-WIDTH BAND

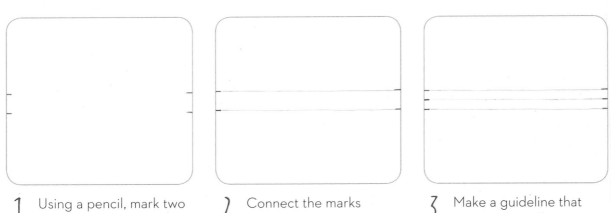

Bands are made of motifs that repeat in a row. Often in a doodle, a band will curve as it wraps around the main form. Practice this version and then begin curving the guidelines for greater 3-D illusion.

1 Using a pencil, mark two distances, 1 inch (2.5cm) and 1½ inches (3.75cm) down from the top of your paper. Make the marks 5 inches (12.5cm) apart.

2 Connect the marks to make two level guidelines.

3 Make a guideline that runs horizontally across the center of the space between the previous guidelines.

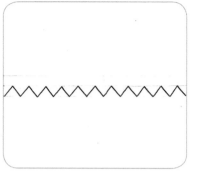

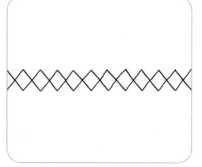

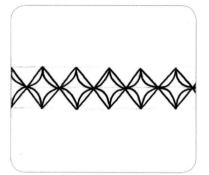

4   Draw a row of zigzagging lines so the alternating tips touch the lower and middle guidelines.

5   Draw another row of zigzagging lines so the tips touch the upper and middle guidelines.

6   Draw curving lines from corner to corner inside the diamond shapes.

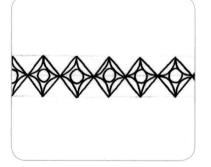

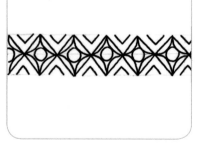

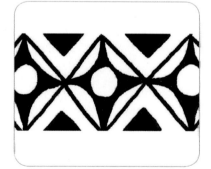

7   Add circles in the spaces at the centers of the diamond shapes.

8   Draw V shapes in the spaces between the diamonds.

9   Color in the small spaces around the circles, and fill in the small Vs to make triangles.

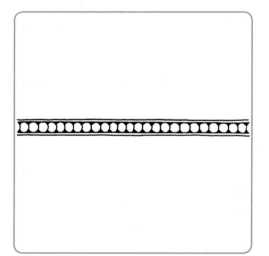

BEADED BAND

This motif has an eye-catching balance of tones. You might see it replicated elsewhere by simply drawing circles between two lines, but this method emphasizes depth with the rhythm of the triangular shadow shapes and the bead curves.

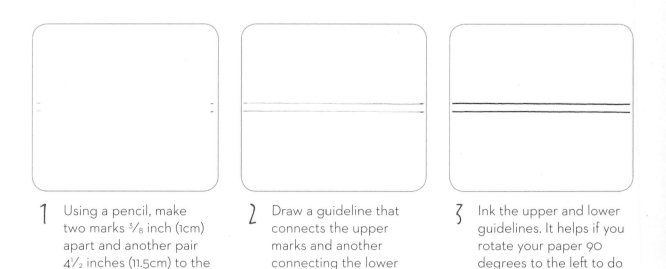

1 Using a pencil, make two marks $3/8$ inch (1cm) apart and another pair $4^1/_2$ inches (11.5cm) to the right.

2 Draw a guideline that connects the upper marks and another connecting the lower marks.

3 Ink the upper and lower guidelines. It helps if you rotate your paper 90 degrees to the left to do this.

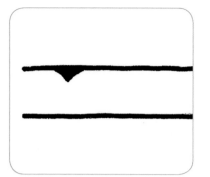

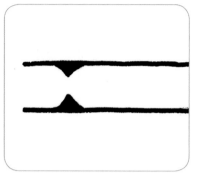

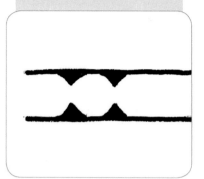

4 Near the left end of the upper guideline, draw a triangular shape with slightly curved sides.

5 Draw another triangular shape that reflects.

6 Ink another pair of triangular shapes to the right of the first two to form a round negative space.

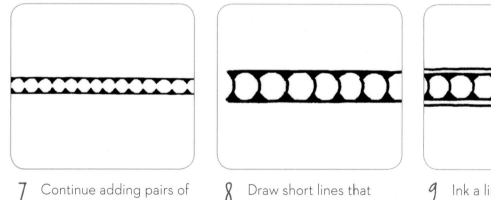

7 Continue adding pairs of triangular shapes to form a row of circular negative spaces.

8 Draw short lines that curve to the right and connect the upper triangle's tip to the lower one.

9 Ink a line above and below the beaded area.

BEADED BAND

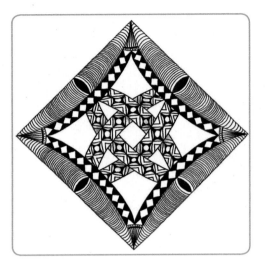

BAND DOODLE

This doodle is a meditation on the petal form. To draw the straight lines of the main shape so they have a freehand look, lay a ruler nearby at the correct angle and use it as a visual guide only.

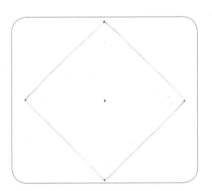

1   Mark the center and then pencil in four dots 2¹⁄₂ inches (6.25cm) above, below, and to either side of the center dot. Connect the outer four dots to make a diamond shape.

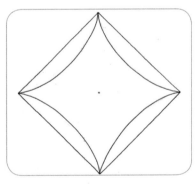

2   Ink the diamond, and draw four curves stretching from corner to adjacent corner.

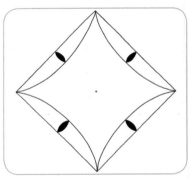

3   Make four petal shapes in the center of the four curved shapes aligned with the center dot.

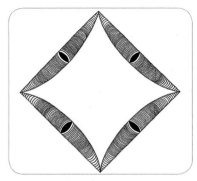

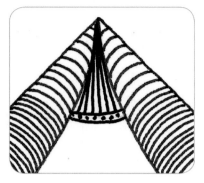

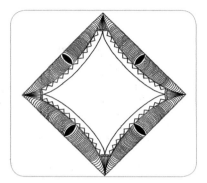

4 Draw curved cross-contour lines on either side of the petal shape spaced farther apart at the corners.

5 In each corner, make a fan shape from two curves, dots, and radiating lines.

6 Draw curves that stretch from one fan to an adjacent fan and then add small triangles pointing inward.

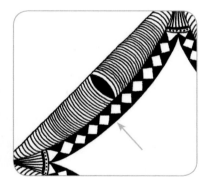

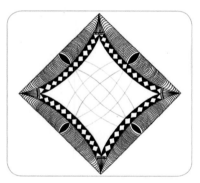

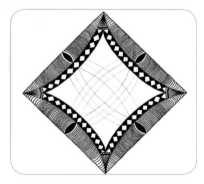

7 Draw outward pointing triangles that touch the tips of the inward pointing triangles, and ink them.

8 Using a pencil, sketch four pairs of curved lines in the shape of petals that curve toward the black petal shapes.

9 Draw a guideline down the center of the space between the pairs of curved lines.

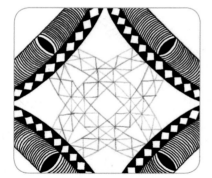

10 Pencil diamond shapes within the pairs of curved lines.

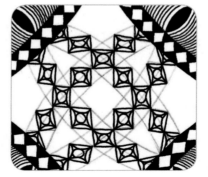

11 Ink the small diamonds, and inside each, make four curved lines and a circle.

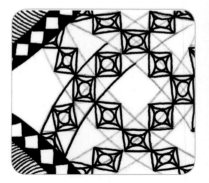

12 Ink the sides of the left curving band, but stop at the inside curve of the top band.

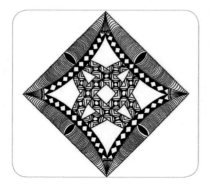

13 Rotate your paper and then ink the rest of the band edges, fill in the spaces around the circles, and draw additional small V shapes.

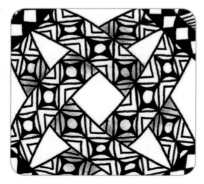

14 With a pencil, shade the overlapping bands where they cross.

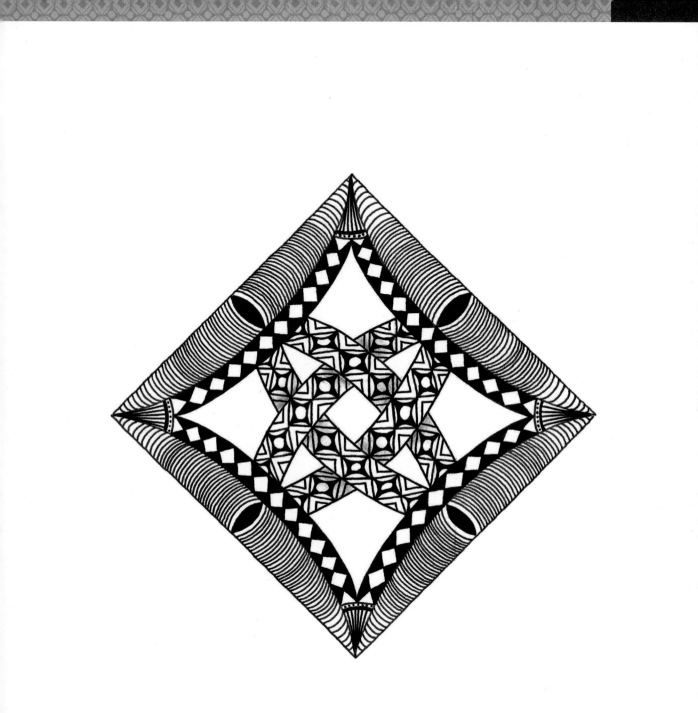

BAND DOODLE

ALTERNATING STRIPES

After drawing the guidelines for this doodle, you can fill in the spaces with any texture or color. This pattern uses a continuous line that demands patience but is a great skill-builder, producing grosgrain ribbon and pinstripe textures.

1 Using a pencil, mark alternating ½-inch (1.25cm) and ¼-inch (.625cm) widths along the top of the page.

2 With a ruler, extend the far right mark to be 2½ inches (6.25cm) long.

3 Starting at the long line, make marks ½ inch (1.25cm) and then ¼ inch (.625cm) apart across the bottom of the page, as in step 1.

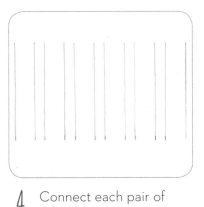

4 Connect each pair of aligned marks with a light pencil guideline.

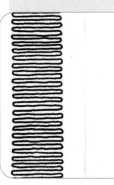

5 Rotate your paper 90 degrees to the right, and fill the top (far left) space with a continuous line texture.

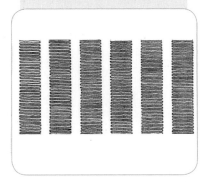

6 Fill all the wider spaces with the continuous line texture.

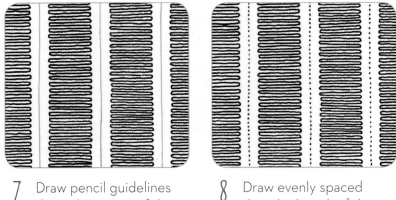

7 Draw pencil guidelines down the center of the narrow spaces.

8 Draw evenly spaced dots the length of the guidelines.

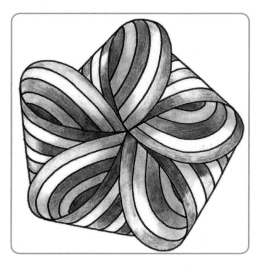

STRIPES DOODLE

Stripes multiply the 3-D effect of a surface that is turning and folding. For this illusion, remember that the edge of every interior stripe that's overlapped continues to curve up to meet the exterior edge of the same stripe.

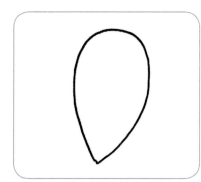

1 In ink, draw a teardrop shape.

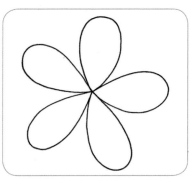

2 Draw four more teardrop shapes that rotate around the center where their tips meet.

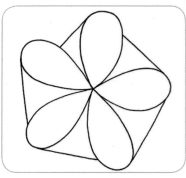

3 Draw a straight line from near the top of each teardrop shape angling downward to touch the side of the adjacent teardrop shape.

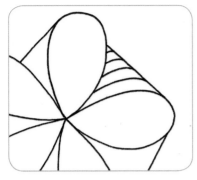

4   Draw lines that repeat the curve of the left edge of a teardrop shape.

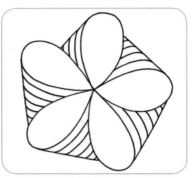

5   Repeat step 4 in all the curved triangular shapes.

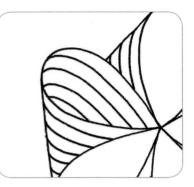

6   Draw lines in one of the teardrop shapes that repeat the curve of the outside edge.

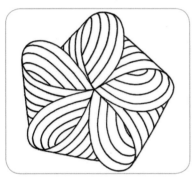

7   Repeat step 6 in the remaining teardrop shapes.

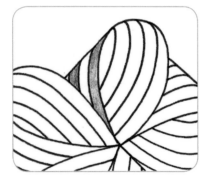

8   With a pencil, shade the first stripe of the upper exterior shape, skip a stripe width, and shade the next.

9   Shade the interior stripes in an alternating pattern to match the exterior stripes.

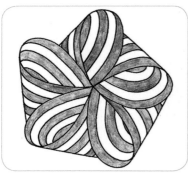 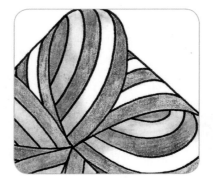 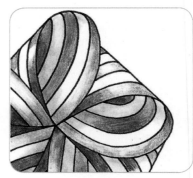

10   Shade all the sections' stripes to alternate in the same way.

11   With a blending stump or your clean fingertip, rub the interior space where it meets the exterior surface.

12   Shade the deepest part of the interior along with exterior crevices. Erase highlights parallel to the outside edge.

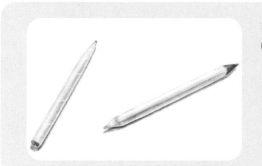

Use a tortillon (left) or a blending stump (right) to soften the pencil shading.

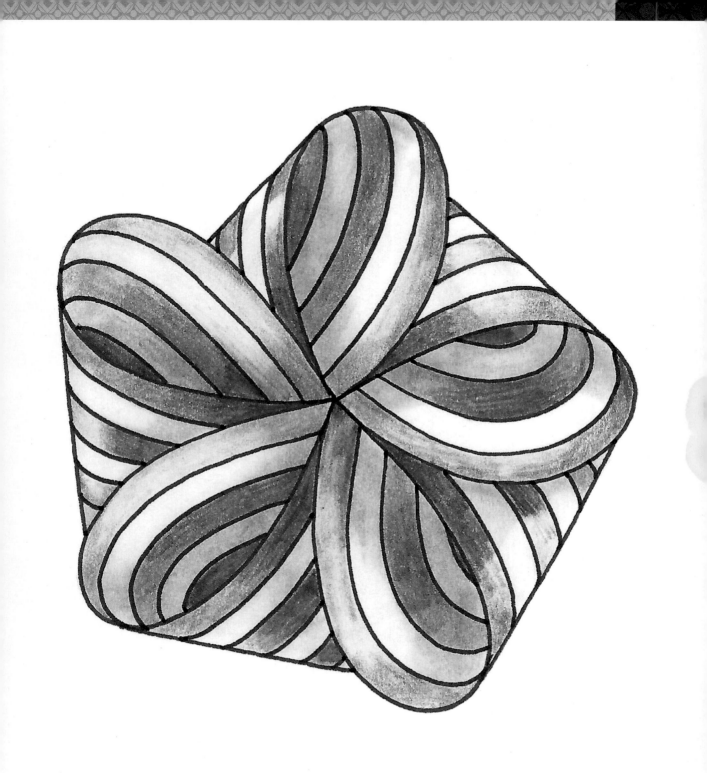

STRIPES DOODLE

9

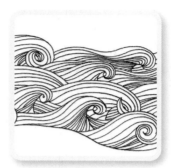

WAVES

The roll of ocean waves is an uneven but continuing cycle. Its soothing power encourages relaxation as well as contemplation. The earliest representation of waves was as spirals and concentric circles by cultures who lived near open water. The graphic pattern of repeating waveforms can draw the viewer into its rhythmic trance.

Although spirals like those representing waves are also used to suggest plants, tendrils, and smoke, when aligned horizontally, they appear as waves. A great variety of pointed and rounded waves are commonly used in graphic works. They can be easily shaped to frame an image or can be a focal point with depth and detail.

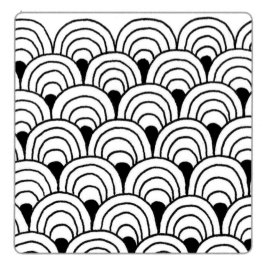

JAPANESE WAVE

This Japanese waveform is a classic and is surprisingly dynamic, sometimes playful, but always gives a doodle a degree of elegance. Drawing the curves to be more circular intensifies the waves' dignified and regal appearance.

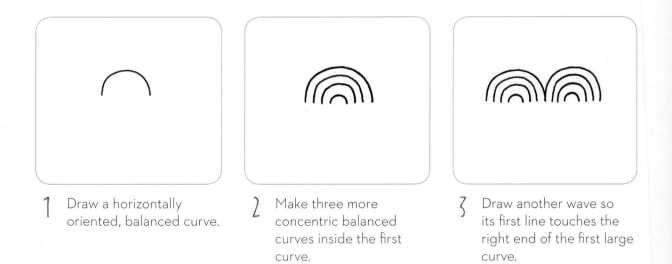

1 Draw a horizontally oriented, balanced curve.

2 Make three more concentric balanced curves inside the first curve.

3 Draw another wave so its first line touches the right end of the first large curve.

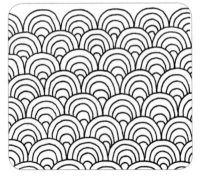

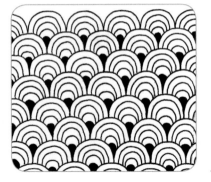

4 Add rows of the tangle upward whose centers fall where the previous row's tangles touch.

5 Enrich the pattern by coloring the centers of the waveforms black.

Simple repetition of the contour of a tangle form is the basis of many reliable patterns. These can take the shapes of Cs, Vs, Us, Js, Os, Xs, boxes, triangles, and irregular shapes. Think of them as ornamental shading: the closer you set the repeats, the darker the resulting value.

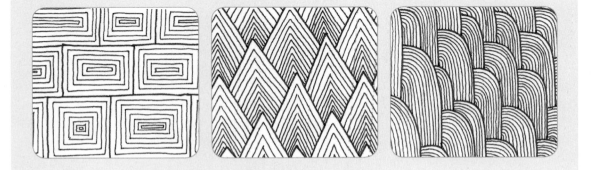

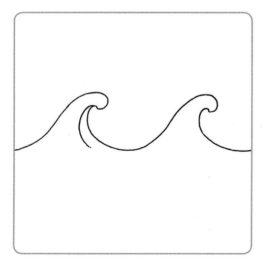

CAPPED WAVE

These slightly curved lines with no wavering create lots of dramatic tension that's offset by tighter curves. This wave has a dignified feel that works well as a framing device.

Take care to avoid smudging what you've already drawn.

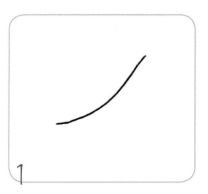

1 Begin by drawing a smooth rising curve while anticipating it will gradually bend and curve down the opposite way.

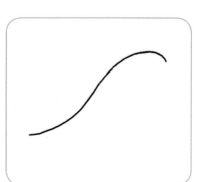

2 Without stopping, curve the line to the right and down.

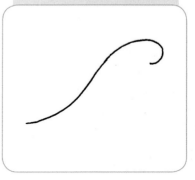

3 Rotate your paper to the right to draw the tight curl with the tip of your pen on the outside of the curl.

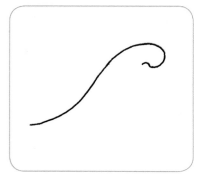

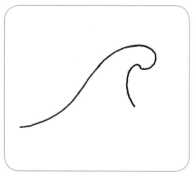

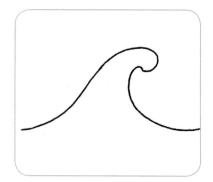

4 Return your paper to level, and draw the tightest part of the curl by smoothly extending your gripping fingers outward.

5 Rotate your paper to the right again, and draw the balanced curve by rotating your wrist.

6 Rotate your paper upside down, and continue the curve.

Draw this detail on every other wave to create alternating rhythm.

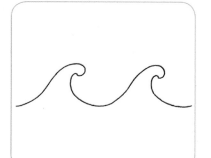

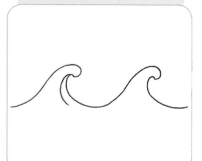

7 Repeat steps 1 through 6 to draw another wave.

8 To create the illusion the wave is turned, add an interior curve that extends down from the cap curl.

UNEVEN WAVE

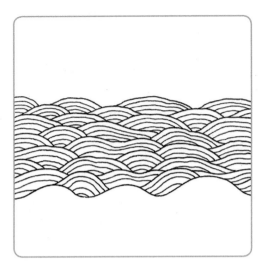

Forms that repeat with subtle variations have great unity while inviting you to look closely. The uneven quality of this wave pattern creates a casual feel and is useful for filling with even tone, texture, and transition.

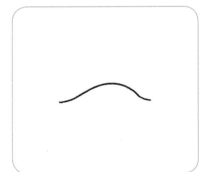

1 Draw a horizontally oriented, nonreflective curve.

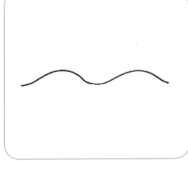

2 Make another curve similar to the first.

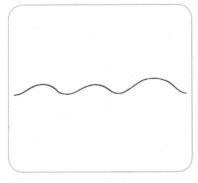

3 Add a section to the contour that's obviously taller.

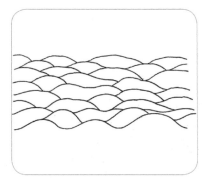

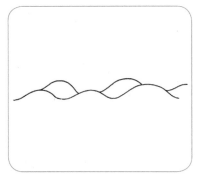

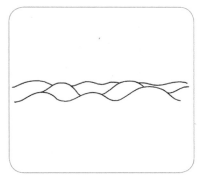

4 Begin the next row back with nonreflective sections that rise where the previous wave contours dipped.

5 Create a different line texture with shallower curves.

6 Fill an area with a blend of the curve types from steps 1 through 5.

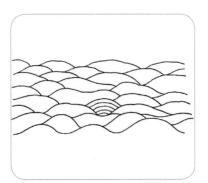

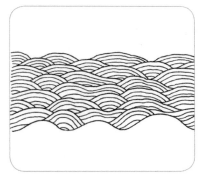

7 Create slightly wavering curves that repeat the outside curve of a waveform with slight variations.

8 Fill each of the waveforms except those created in steps 1 through 3 with curves, as in step 7.

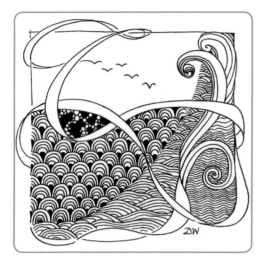

WAVE DOODLE

The frame of a doodle is activated when interior elements touch or overlap it. In this case, the flowing ribbon creates depth while suggesting movement with curving lines that appear to float over the image's surface.

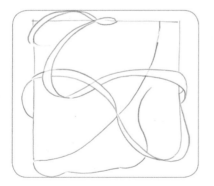

1 Using a pencil, begin by drawing the main shape and sections.

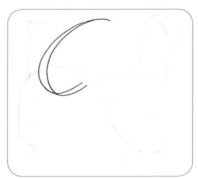

2 In ink, start the ribbon by drawing the near edge with a C-shape curve and then two more curves.

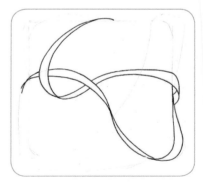

3 Continue drawing the ribbon with curves. Rotate your paper between strokes to draw the curves more easily.

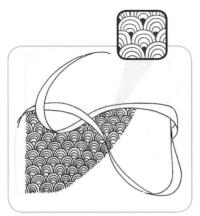

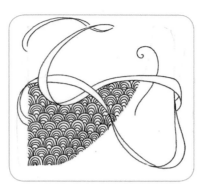

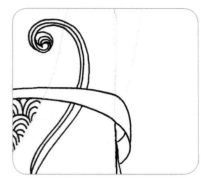

4 Fill the lower-left section with the **Japanese wave** tangle.

5 Complete the upper ribbon and then add a curling line that's overlapped by the ribbon.

6 Embellish the depth of the curl with lines that run parallel to the first curve and then touch it.

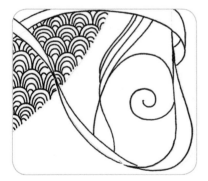

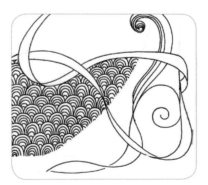

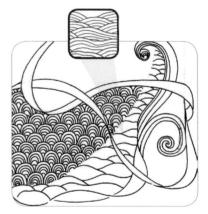

7 Extend the curling line with curves that appear to twist in the lower area.

8 Add another twist to the lower ribbon with an S curve and two shorter curving lines.

9 Fill the lower-right section with the main contours of the **uneven wave** tangle.

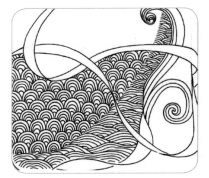

10 Add the repeating interior lines of the uneven wave tangle in every section.

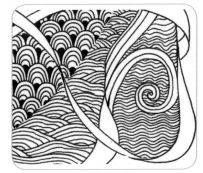

11 Fill the small area at the lower right with repeating wavy lines.

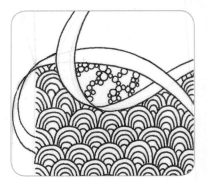

12 Draw small circles grouped in connecting, curving clusters.

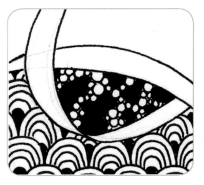

13 Color the areas between the circle clusters black.

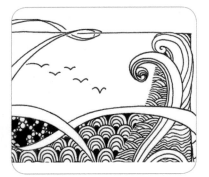

14 Add another curling form at the upper right and then draw curving V shapes (birds) that align with the end of the ribbon.

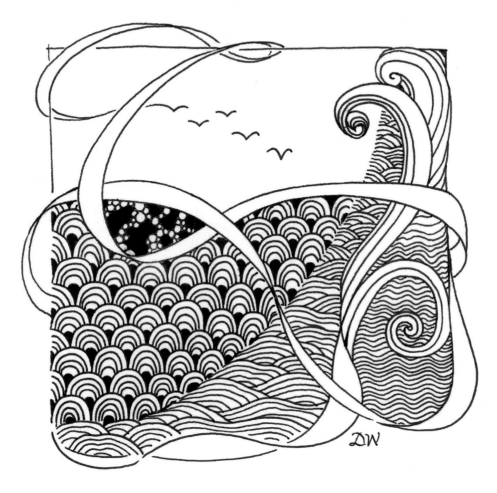

WAVE DOODLE

10

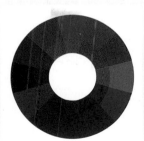

TONE AND COLOR

Understanding how tones and colors work helps you have more control over illusions in your doodles. There are three basic aspects of color. First, is *hue*. Hue is the color family it belongs to. Next is its *value*, or how dark or light it is. The third is the color's *intensity*, or how saturated or bright the color is.

Black ink is *achromatic,* or without color in relation to hues, which are chromatic. Sunlight's pure white appearance is made of rays of all the hues. Spectral colors are visible when sunlight is projected through water in the form of a rainbow or through a prism. These spectral hues are illustrated in the color wheel. The outside ring displays the pure hues, and the interior ring shows shades created by adding black.

VALUE AND CONTRAST

Value is so critical to expression in 2-D visual art that some artists see achromatic tone as rich a color as any spectral hue. Black ink pens and graphite or charcoal pencils all create achromatic tone, and each has unusual and exciting possibilities for doodles. Creating value scales is helpful for gaining tonal control and learning the value range of different mediums.

Each drawing and shading medium has an inherent range of values that's key to its expressive power. Graphite pencils are excellent for creating pale to midrange values, but their darkest values aren't as dark as black ink.

Graphite black (left) and ink black (right).

Value scale done in pencil.

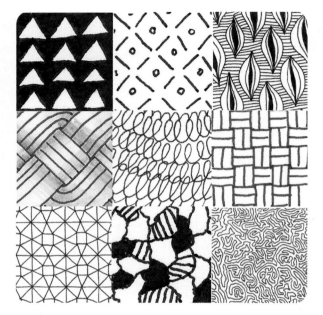

Tangle tones.

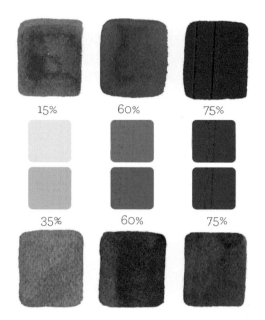

15% 60% 75%

35% 60% 75%

Primary and secondary triads compared.

Conversely, it's difficult to create pale tones with ink pens, but their darkest black is very rich. So combining them by inking and then shading with pencil produces a wider achromatic range for doodling.

The colors used in watercolors, colored pencils, and markers have inherent value range relating to the pigments from which they're made. Compare the values of the three primary colors (yellow, red, and blue), and you'll see the great difference in range of the individual hues and that this triad, or group of three, has greater inherent range than secondary or tertiary colors because the yellow is so pale. The palest tones of the two triads can be tinted with water or white to very pale, as can the blue and violet hues.

The primary triad has greater range when mixing colors because it's possible to make close equivalents of all secondary and tertiary colors with proportions of high-quality lemon yellow, quinacridone red, and phthalo blue watercolors.

BASIC COLOR THEORY

᧬ᩬᬇᩢᩢ

When using color, it may be difficult to know what color to start with and then what colors to add next. It's natural to choose a color based on favoritism or inclination, but there are also ways to use colors for their effectiveness.

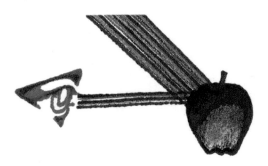

Subtractive color.

The color wheel displays the hues of the spectrum as they relate to colored pigment applied to a surface. It explains the subtractive color system, in which color is transmitted through the eyes to the brain, which interprets the remaining light waves after some have been absorbed (subtracted) into the viewed object's surface.

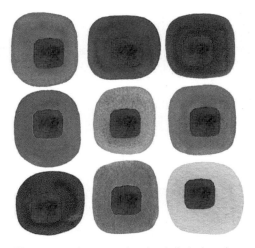

The same red appears bright, dull, dark, pale, warm, or cool in relation to the adjacent color.

When you doodle, color is palpable, and you may have feelings about a particular color that can't be found on a chart. But as you paint or shade, eventually using colors that now are unusual to you, try to see them also for their effectiveness to create unity, to create a visual path, and to be balanced. As you improve these aspects of doodling, your self-expression will grow.

The primary colors (red, yellow, and blue) and the secondary colors (orange, green, and purple) are color triads that have unity built in. They're a good place to begin your experiments with color. Create a doodle that uses only shades and tints of the primary colors and then try one that only uses the secondary triad. This helps build your confidence to use and blend colors well.

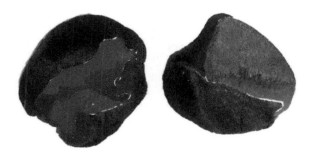

Color triads.

When you doodle with triads, you may notice how color has warmth or coolness. While red is usually warm, some reds contain more blue, making them appear cooler when next to a red with an orange cast. Conversely, when next to ultramarine blue, manganese blue looks warmer, although blue appears cool in relation to red and yellow.

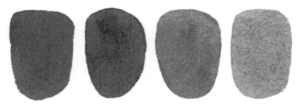

Color temperature: cool red, warm red; manganese blue, ultramarine blue.

Generally, warm colors are on the top half of the color wheel and cool colors are on the lower half.

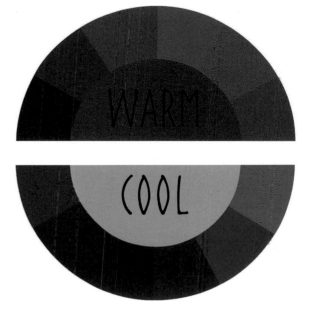

WORKING WITH COMPLEMENTARY COLORS

Colors can be arranged to emphasize or deemphasize the effect of another hue. The color wheel helps make more sense of relational color like this. It displays the pure hues of the spectrum and is a starting point for choosing colors so they work effectively.

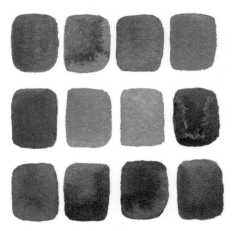

Some analogous color sets.

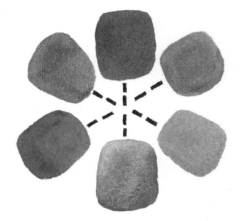

Complementary pairs.

One important job colors can perform in an image is creating unity. *Analogous color* is made from those that are side by side on the color wheel, like yellow, orange, and red. These colors go together easily, and you can achieve beautiful effects with a simple choice like this where no single color stands out. However, to emphasize one color over others requires greater contrast.

Colors that contrast in hue are *complementary*. These colors enhance each other's vibrancy and are positioned directly across from each other on the color wheel. The color with the most complementary contrast in relation to orange, for example, is blue; the color opposite green is red; and yellow is more vibrant paired with violet.

CHAPTER 10: TONE AND COLOR

You can achieve greater vibrancy by pairing color complements in a doodle. However, colors are often used in a less-pure form than the spectral colors you see on the color wheel. They're also used in various proportions to each other to sometimes create balance or enliven another color. A little red, for example, can bring a gray-green area to life.

Usually pure hues are weakened slightly to be less intense. Many artists' colors are already modified to popular color choices, but mixing colors from pure primaries strengthens your understanding of how colors relate. Add small amounts of a color's complement to weaken its saturation and create a range of new colors.

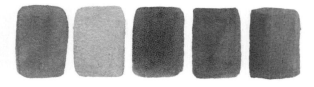

Mix a complementary pair to make less-saturated colors.

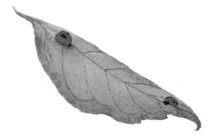

A small amount of a color's complement creates intensity and balance.

Mixing quinacridone red and phthalo green produces a whole set of colors and greenish or reddish black.

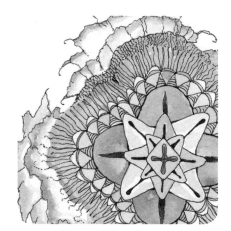

Mixing complementary colors creates a range of colorful grays.

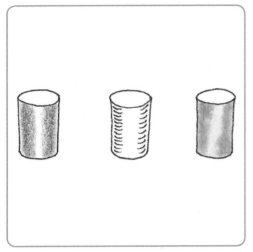

Modeling shading in pencil (left), pen (center), and watercolors (right).

SHADING WITH COLOR

You can add a realistic-looking rounding effect to cylinders and round objects with a shading technique called *modeling*. Shade the sides where the form appears to turn away, and as you shade the length of the form's edges, leave a highlight at the center part of the illusion that appears closest to you.

> Don't apply the color force-fully. Allow the wet surface to pull the paint from the tip of your brush.

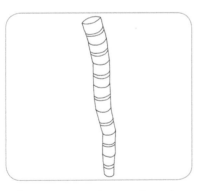

1 Draw a column of reeds.

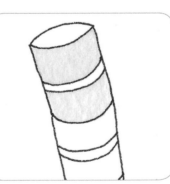

2 With a #4 round watercolor brush, wet the top two sections of the tangle with a pale green color. This is called *priming*.

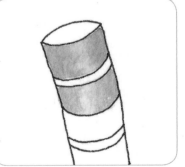

3 While the color is wet but not puddling, add a darker green to the sides with gentle touches.

CHAPTER 10: TONE AND COLOR

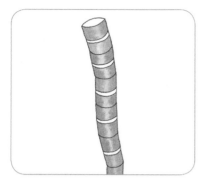

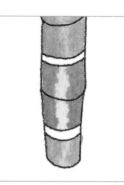

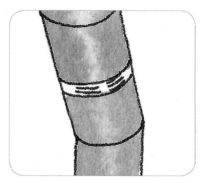

4 Shade all the tangle sections as in steps 2 and 3, except for the narrow bands.

5 If the highlight turns out stark with hard edges, it's due to the priming being too dry when the modeling shading was added. Rewet the sections, blot the color away, and start over.

6 Begin inking the narrow bands by making short curves. Leave a gap in the center.

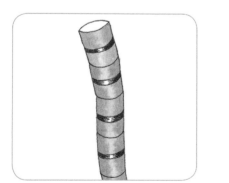

Edges are important when you shade. Keep the transition from the dark sides to the highlight soft to support the effect of a curving surface.

7 Shade the sides of the bands black.

CREATING A GRADATION

To create a gradation, or an even shading from dark to light, begin in the center of the upper area and work outward and downward. Keep the edges of the shading sections soft, shade the darkest part last, and alternate between side-to-side and vertical stroke patterns.

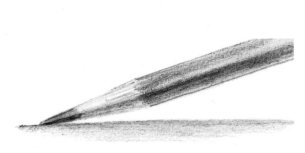

Angle for pale shading.

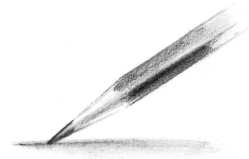

Angle for dark shading.

Notice the angled sides of the shaded section.

1 Using a pencil, and beginning in the center of the upper area, make several left-to-right strokes.

2 Continue making soft, sweeping strokes in one direction that overlap the first group and spread to the right.

3 Begin transitioning to the lower, lighter area.

4 Make shorter strokes using less pressure to soften the edges and eliminate some unevenness.

5 Make more sweeping strokes like at the start but with even less pressure.

6 Shade to the bottom edge. Don't shade to the side edges yet.

7 Make short strokes with light pressure to fill the parts that aren't shaded yet.

8 When a stroke stands out as too dark, shade the lighter area around it with more pressure to make the tones even.

9 Rotate your paper 90 degrees to the left for the final shading. Make short strokes in the darkest area.

10 Continue making short strokes in the lower area with very light pressure.

11 Make short strokes with more pressure in the upper area to darken and even out the tones.

12 In one final pass, shade with even more pressure at the top and transition to very light pressure at bottom.

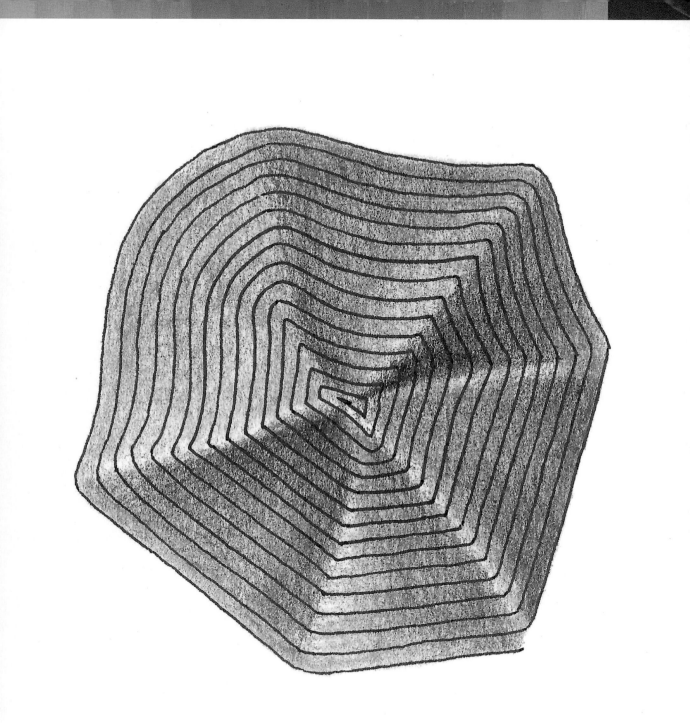

CREATING A GRADATION

11

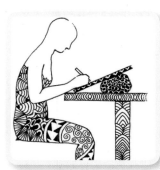

ASSEMBLING PATTERNS INTO SHAPES

Doodling is the act of drawing patterns into a shape. It's a process of coming to a design gradually and enjoying the course of it unfolding. You'll often sketch a main shape when you start a doodle, but it's only a starting point, and you'll alter it as you make choices and simply draw lines and shapes. You learn more about doodling every time you create one, and your progress and style will develop in a unique way. Eventually, you will choose or create patterns you *feel* rather than patterns you know work.

The doodles in this chapter show you the different directions your drawings can take—sometimes with figurative elements, often purely pattern. Re-create them to understand how the process works until you begin to find your own way. You'll discover your own amazing doodles when your mind is calm and your imagination is flowing.

FITTING SHAPES

This doodle is based on shapes found in seashells. You can follow the method of this doodle by finding your own shells and drawing some shapes you see or copying the tangles used here.

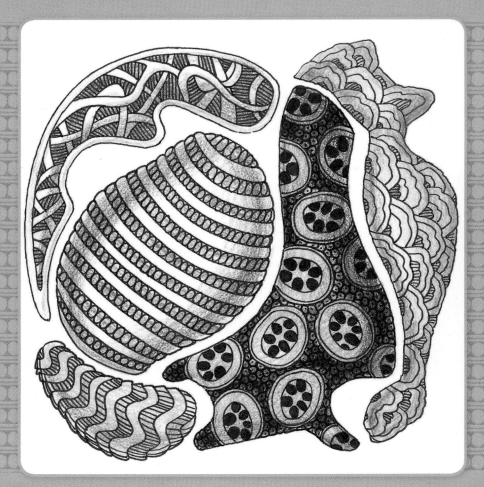

1 Draw the inspiration shape—in this case, the contour of a shell.

2 Add other shapes around the first one with narrow to wider spaces between them.

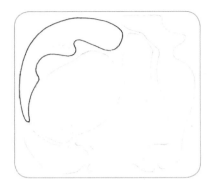

3 Begin the ink stage by outlining the upper-left shape.

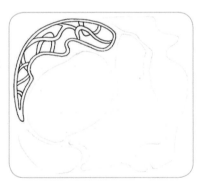

4 Draw another outline inside the first one, and add tangle elements.

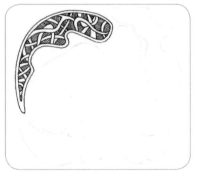

5 Draw more tangle elements to fill the space, and shade in the gaps with hatch marks.

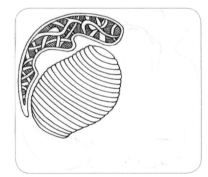

6 Next, draw curving, cross-contour lines across the inspiration shape, and round the ends slightly.

FITTING SHAPES

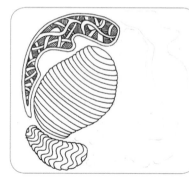

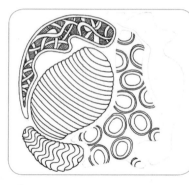

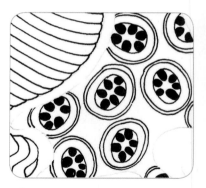

7   Similar to the previous shape, draw cross-contour lines on the next shape but make them wavy for variety.

8   Draw repeating concentric ovals across the next shape.

9   Fill the innermost ovals with black, seedlike shapes.

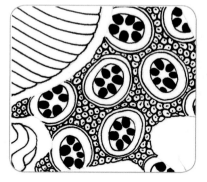

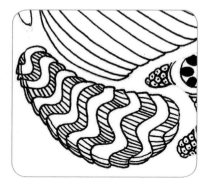

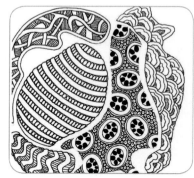

10   To fill in the background of the shape, add small, irregular circles with center dots.

11   Shade alternating parts of the smallest shape with hatch marks.

12   Fill in the last shape with undulating waves running the length of the shape, and outline it. On the inspiration shape, draw repeating ovals in every other row.

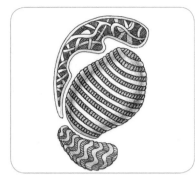

13   Color the spaces in the top shape blue and the two shapes below it pale magenta and pale yellow. Shade the shadows purple and turquoise.

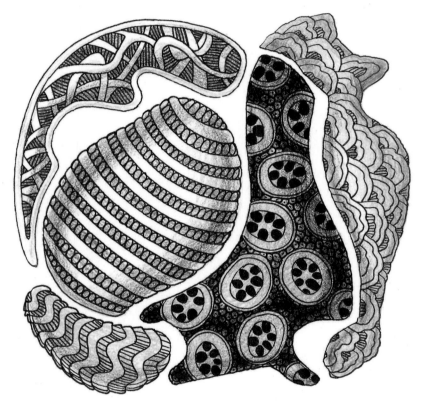

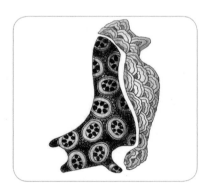

14   Color the largest shape pale yellow and pale red. Between the ovals, use deep red. Color the last shape turquoise with violet shading.

STARS

Dark tones help pale tones look even paler through value contrast.
The illusion of starlight is heightened in this doodle by emphasizing
portions of white paper and by contrasting them with a dark tangle.

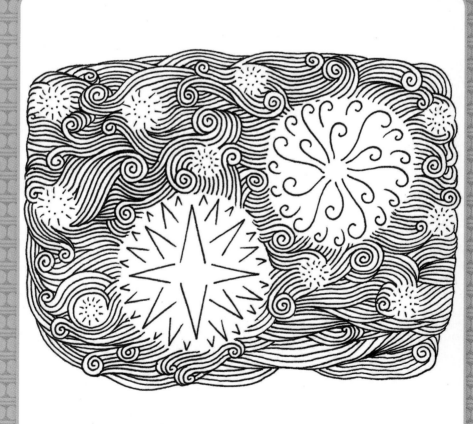

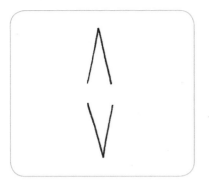

1 Begin creating a large star with two V shapes, each about ¾ inch (2cm) tall.

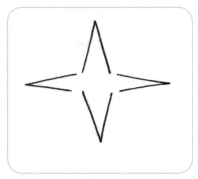

2 Draw another pair of V shapes oriented horizontally toward the first two.

3 Add two pairs of Vs in the center of the spaces between the previous Vs.

4 Draw eight more small Vs centered in the spaces between the previous V shapes.

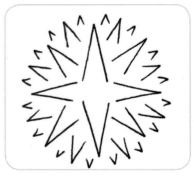

5 Finally, add 16 small Vs in the remaining spaces between the previous V shapes.

6 Begin a star with curling lines that radiate from a blank center point.

7　Fit shorter curling parts in the spaces between the previous lines.

8　Complete the star by fitting more curls in the spaces between the previous curls.

9　Draw a new little star made of a ring of dots with short lines that radiate outward.

10　Add more of the small stars, being careful not to align them three in a row.

11　Start shading the sky by drawing a curving line with a spiral at one end.

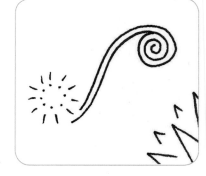

12　Add another curling line parallel to the previous one.

 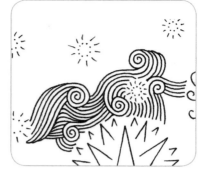 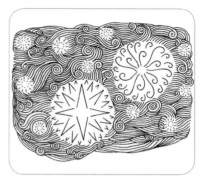

13 Add more lines to build out from the previous sky curl. Begin another sky curl a short distance away from the first.

14 Tie together the sky curls with curving and wavy lines.

15 Continue with the sky curl pattern to surround all the stars.

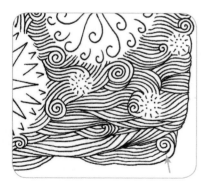

16 Add more lines to refine the sky's edge so it's smoother, more balanced, and not distracting.

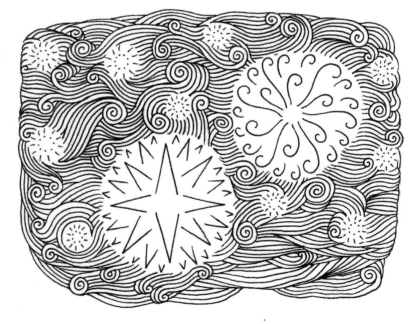

PAISLEY

When doodling a paisley, emphasize its elegant S curve. Fashionable in fifteenth-century Persia, the *boteh* (bush) shape is also associated with Paisley, Scotland, where textiles with the popular motif were manufactured and exported in the 1800s.

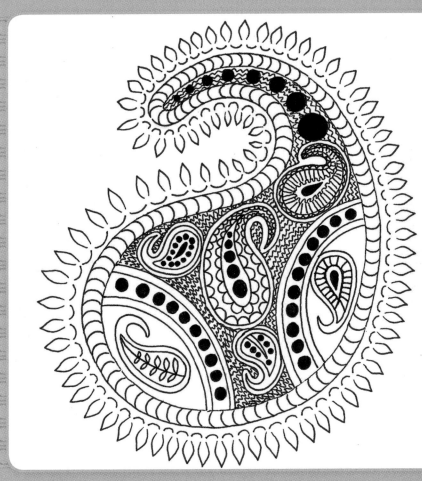

1 Using a pencil, sketch a paisley shape about 6 inches (15cm) tall.

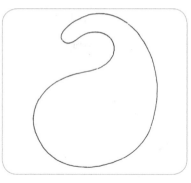

2 Trace the shape in pen.

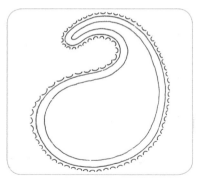

3 Outline the shape with scallops and add an interior contour.

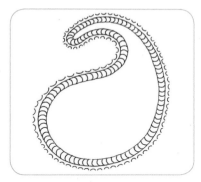

4 Fit scallops between the two contours.

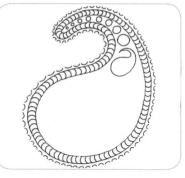

5 Draw a few small to larger circles in the main shape and then add a small paisley contour.

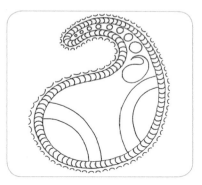

6 Fit pairs of curving lines low in the interior to create bands and almond-shape sections.

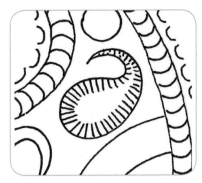

7   Fill the interior with paisleys. Inside the upper paisley, draw short lines that point inward.

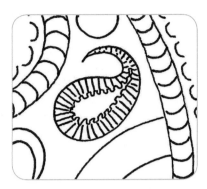

8   Add a wavy line around the interior of the small paisley.

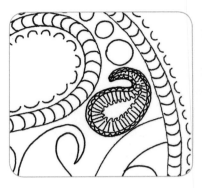

9   Draw half circles and then an outline around the upper paisley.

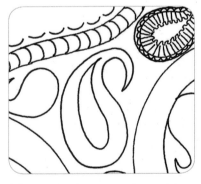

10   In the next paisley, add an interior contour line.

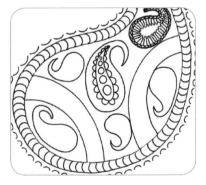

11   Fill the shape with circles, and outline it with half circles.

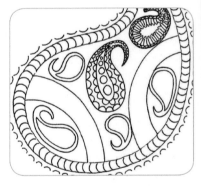

12   Add more half circles to complete the pattern.

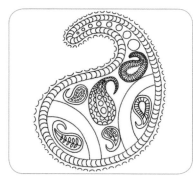

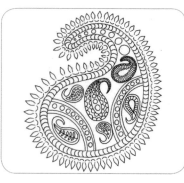

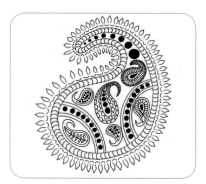

13 Decorate the other paisleys with pattern variations.

14 Fill the curving bands with circles. Draw leaf shapes outside the scalloped exterior.

15 Color in the circles and teardrop shapes with black ink.

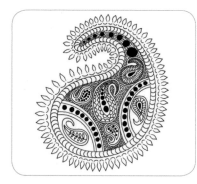

16 Add wavy lines to shade the main interior section.

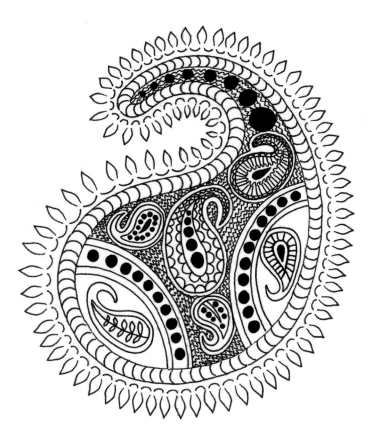

PAISLEY

FOREST

This doodle contrasts many subtle vertical elements with the strong horizontals of the tree branch and the woodland hills. You use a variety of tangles and shading to create a dense tapestry of woodland growth.

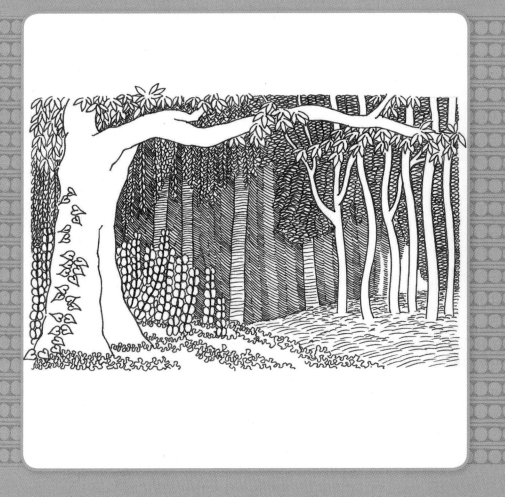

1 Using a pencil, sketch a
rectangle 5 inches tall
by 7½ inches wide (12 by
19cm).

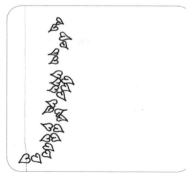

2 Switch to a .45mm black
ink pen, and draw heart-
shape ivy leaves in pairs
on the left side in an
irregular line.

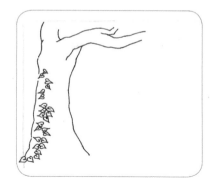

3 Add contours of the
tree, allowing small gaps
occasionally.

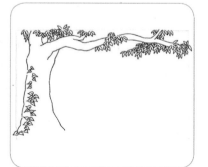

4 Using a tri-leaf tangle,
fill in the upper area of
the tree with groups of
leaves.

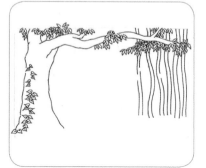

5 Draw tree trunks at the
right with pairs of wavy
lines and a few gaps.

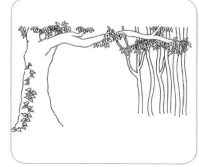

6 Add three branches at
the gaps, overlapping
the trunks slightly and
curving upward.

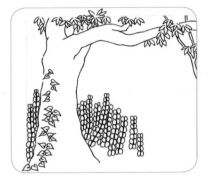

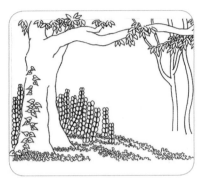

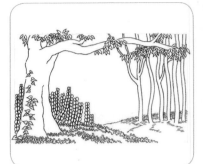

7 Draw pairs of stacked ovals from the ground up to create weedy growth behind the foreground tree.

8 With a squiggle tangle, create horizontal texture that gradually curves downward to the right.

9 Shade the ground beneath the group of trees at the right with shallow curves.

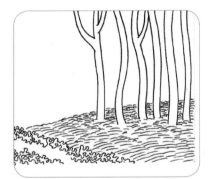

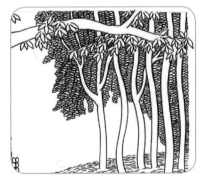

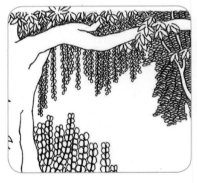

10 Add more shading curves to fill in the ground below the trees at the right.

11 Create the leaf texture behind the trees at the right by repeating connected horizontal figure eights downward.

12 Draw hanging vines with a repeating teardrop tangle.

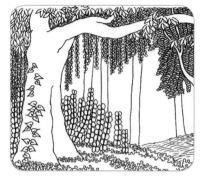

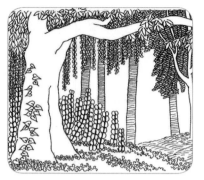

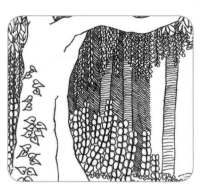

13 Add four more tree trunks in the background with pairs of vertical lines.

14 Shade the background tree trunks with slightly wavy horizontal cross-contour lines.

15 Begin shading the background around the trees using diagonal marks angling downward to the right.

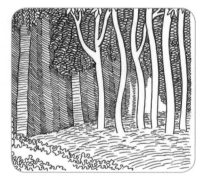

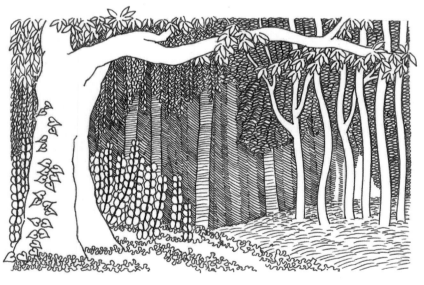

16 Complete the background shading, leaving some white space to indicate a distant clearing.

MANDALA

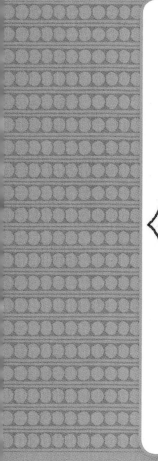

This form of rotational symmetry is constructed on a grid of lines that radiate from a center like spokes. Rotate your paper as you draw, keeping the grid line of the part you're drawing vertical.

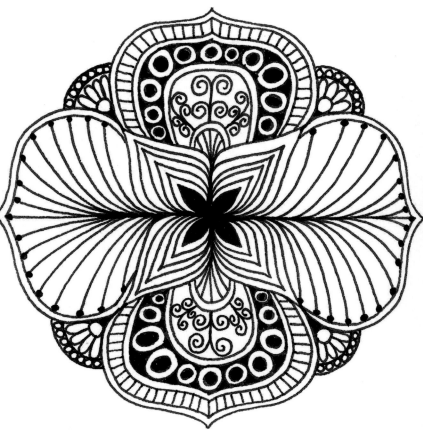

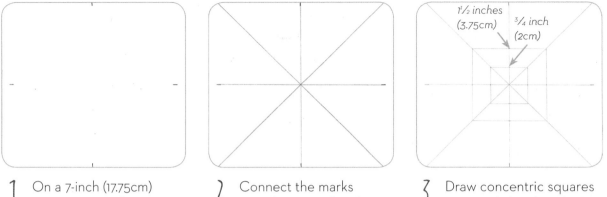

1 On a 7-inch (17.75cm) square piece of paper, mark the midpoint of each edge. (If you're drawing a mandala on irregular-size paper, simply draw a square first.)

2 Connect the marks to make vertical and horizontal midpoints. Then draw lines connecting the corners. Use a ruler if you want to draw the grid accurately.

3 Draw concentric squares at ¾ inch (2cm) and 1½ inches (3.75cm) out from the center.

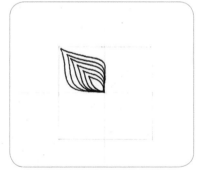

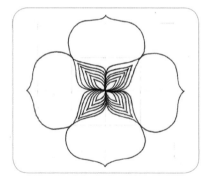

4 Draw a nested leaf tangle aligned with the upper-left diagonal, inside the smaller square.

5 Repeat the nested leaf tangle on all diagonals.

6 Draw leaf shapes made of two reflecting curves that come to a point at the vertical axis.

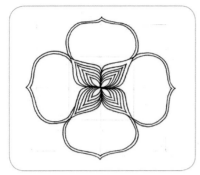

7 | Nest a second leaf contour inside each of the first.

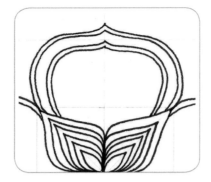

8 | Draw a smaller pair of leaf contours.

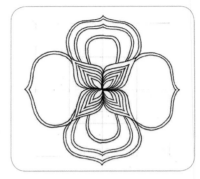

9 | Draw a U shape made of a pair of contours.

Draw the centermost double circle first.

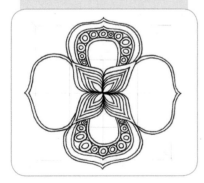

10 | On the upper and lower leaves, fill the space between the inner pairs of contours with repeating double circles.

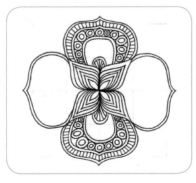

11 | Again working on only the upper and lower leaves, draw a small half-circle double contour. Fill it and the outer gap with shading lines.

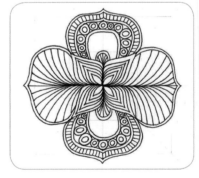

12 | Fill the left and right leaf shapes with curves that repeat progressively more outward.

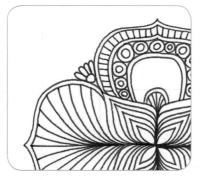 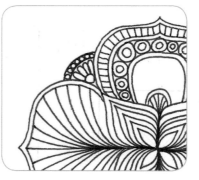 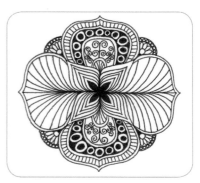

13 Place small flowers made of a small circle and four lobes in the gaps between the leaves.

14 Add beading by drawing a curve, small circles, and an outside curve to enclose the beading.

15 Fill the remaining gaps with a tendril motif. Color the centers and gaps of the parts with black ink.

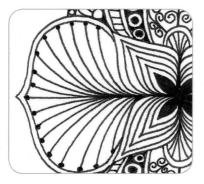

16 Add accent dots to the ends of the curving lines of the horizontal leaves.

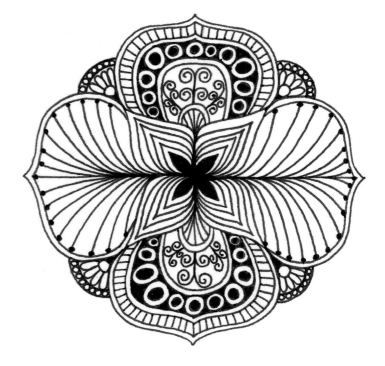

BOXES

Pick a nice piece of textured paper, and prepare to relax as you practice being in alignment and balanced. With this doodle, you have the opportunity to consider your work from many angles and pair shaded colors with delicate pen work.

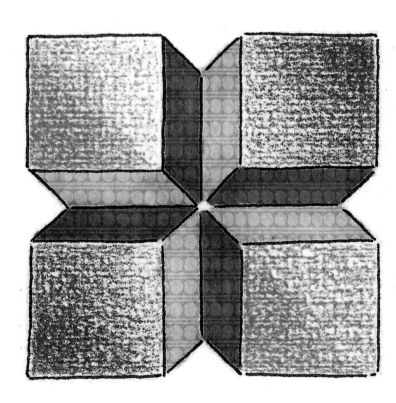

1 Draw a ³/₄-inch (2cm) square. Rotate your paper to check its balance.

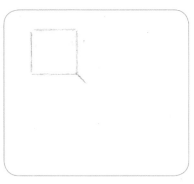

2 When the square is refined, draw a short diagonal line extending from the bottom-right corner.

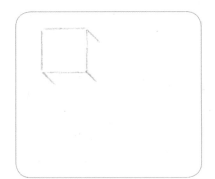

3 Draw two more short diagonal lines parallel to the first one in the top-right and bottom-left corners.

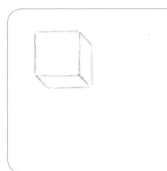

4 Draw a vertical and a horizontal line to close the shape.

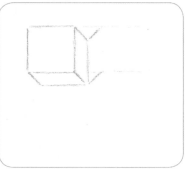

5 Draw two more diagonal lines mirroring the first ones and aligned with the horizontal edges.

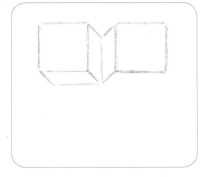

6 Draw a square that mirrors the first. Rotate your paper to check for any imbalance.

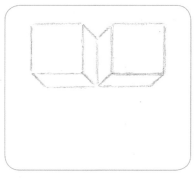

7   Complete the lower section of the right cube to mirror the left cube.

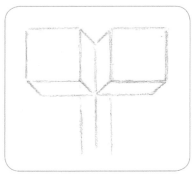

8   Draw three lines that reflect and align with the ones you drew with the first two cubes.

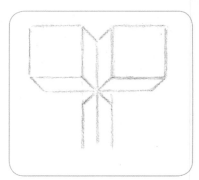

9   Draw two short diagonal lines that align with the ones on the first two cubes and cross at 90 degrees.

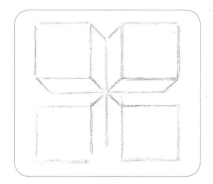

10   Draw two more squares that are balanced and touch the short diagonal lines.

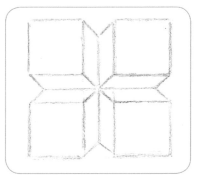

11   Draw two more short diagonal lines that repeat the angles of the previous two.

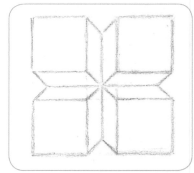

12   Refine the squares and diagonals to be balanced and reflect evenly.

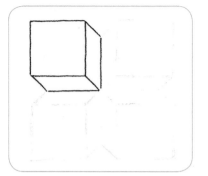

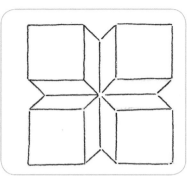

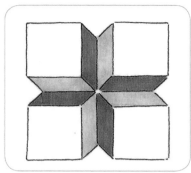

13 When the cubes appear to reflect, trace the upper-left cube in black ink.

14 Trace the rest of the lines carefully with black ink.

15 Color the parallelograms in alternating brown and gray markers.

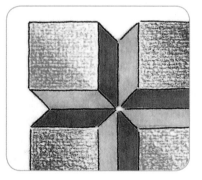

16 Shade the squares with colored pencils to create tonal gradations. Repeat the motif to create a larger field of the pattern.

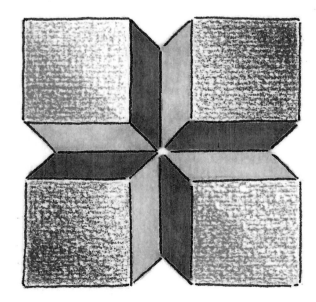

LOOPS

The method for creating this illusion of looping, knotted string is addictively fun and simplified when you realize it's an alternating pattern. Rotate your paper to find the best angle as you trace the lines.

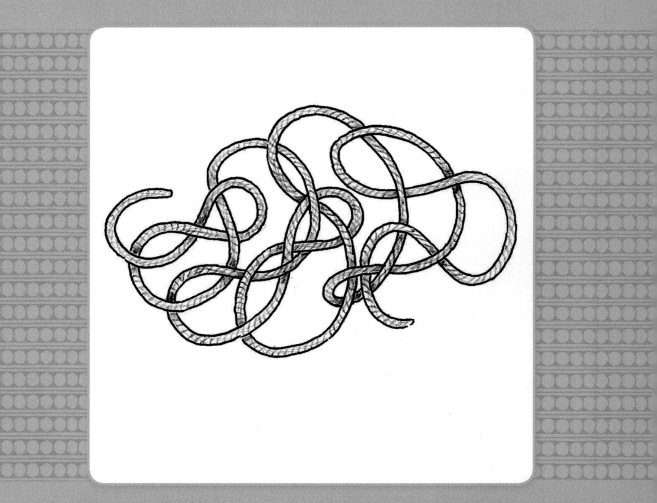

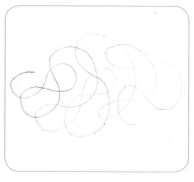

1 Using a pencil, draw a looping line.

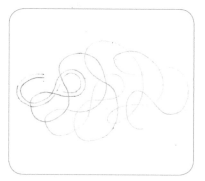

2 Draw a second line parallel to the first to widen it.

3 While drawing the second line, take care to maintain the same distance between the two lines.

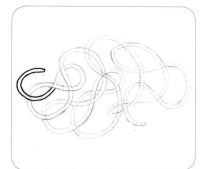

4 Begin tracing the lines in pen starting at the left end.

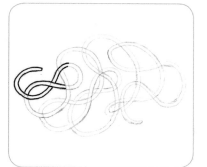

5 To create the illusion of the overlapping loops, stop the lines where they pass under another pair of lines.

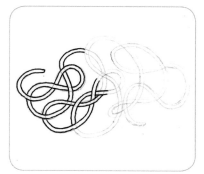

6 Draw the string illusion to overlap and then pass under, and repeat this sequence.

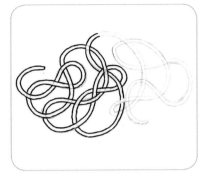

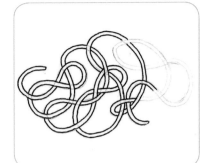

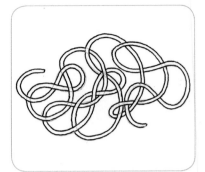

7   At complex areas, remember to draw the overlapping lines first and then those passing under.

8   It's good to have sections where the string takes unexpected turns.

9   Take the same care maintaining the width of the string as you complete the tracing.

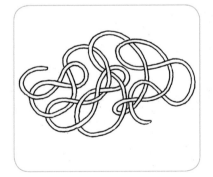

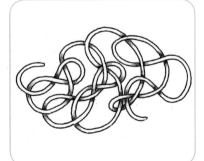

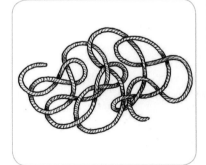

10   Erase the initial pencil lines with a kneaded eraser.

11   Using your pencil again, shade the two sides of the string that pass under an overlapping section.

12   Draw diagonal cross-contour lines to suggest the illusion of wound string.

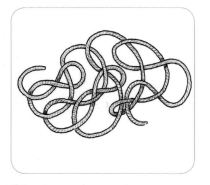

13 Draw diagonal cross-contour lines that cross over the previous ones in the opposite direction.

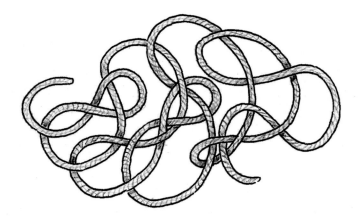

FRAME

Create frames with character using panels with corner and edging details. If you doodle this frame in your sketchbook, you can cut out the center white rectangle to frame a portion of the page beneath.

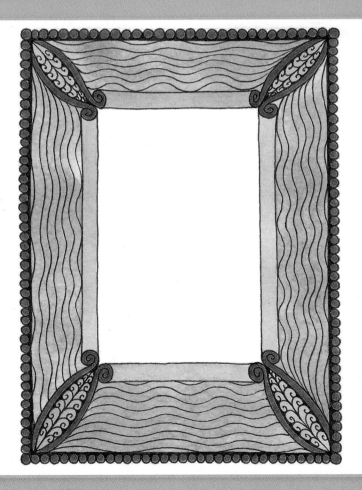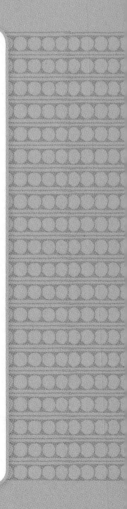

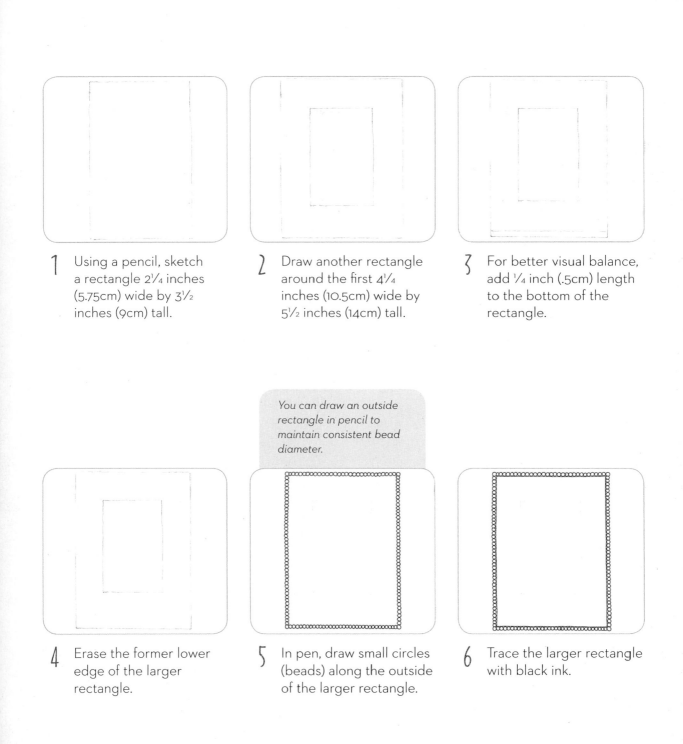

1   Using a pencil, sketch a rectangle 2¼ inches (5.75cm) wide by 3½ inches (9cm) tall.

2   Draw another rectangle around the first 4¼ inches (10.5cm) wide by 5½ inches (14cm) tall.

3   For better visual balance, add ¼ inch (.5cm) length to the bottom of the rectangle.

You can draw an outside rectangle in pencil to maintain consistent bead diameter.

4   Erase the former lower edge of the larger rectangle.

5   In pen, draw small circles (beads) along the outside of the larger rectangle.

6   Trace the larger rectangle with black ink.

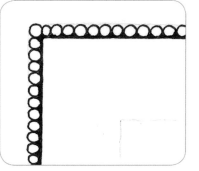

7 Color the spaces between the large rectangle line and the bottoms of the beads black.

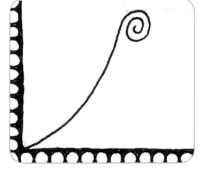

8 Draw a curve upward from the lower-left corner that ends in a spiral at the edge of the smaller rectangle.

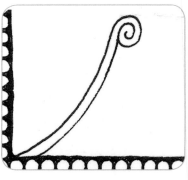

9 Draw a curve down from the spiral back to the corner.

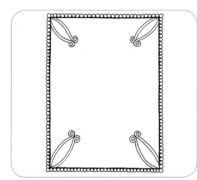

10 Repeat the corner detail as a reflection, and repeat both **curve-and-spiral** doodle in all the corners.

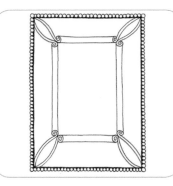

11 Connect the spirals with lines to create the illusion of scroll edges.

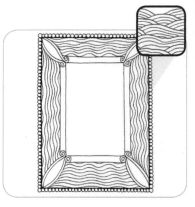

12 Draw a modified **wave** tangle running the length of the frame's panels.

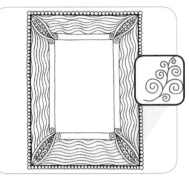

13 Draw a **tendril** tangle in the corner spaces.

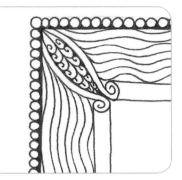

14 Color the small spaces around the tendrils black.

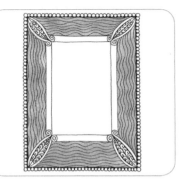

15 Using watercolors, paint the frame panels a pinkish red.

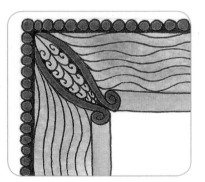

16 Color the beads and corner details with brown marker, and paint the interiors pale green.

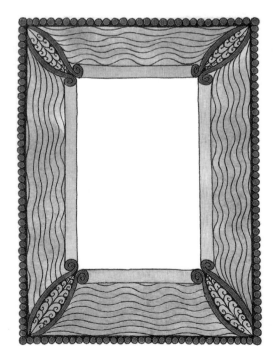

FLOWERS

Doodles are inventions of shape. Likewise, doodling flowers is a visual game in which simply changing size, contour, and texture produces a surprising variety. These doodled flowers are based mainly on a perennial favorite: daisies.

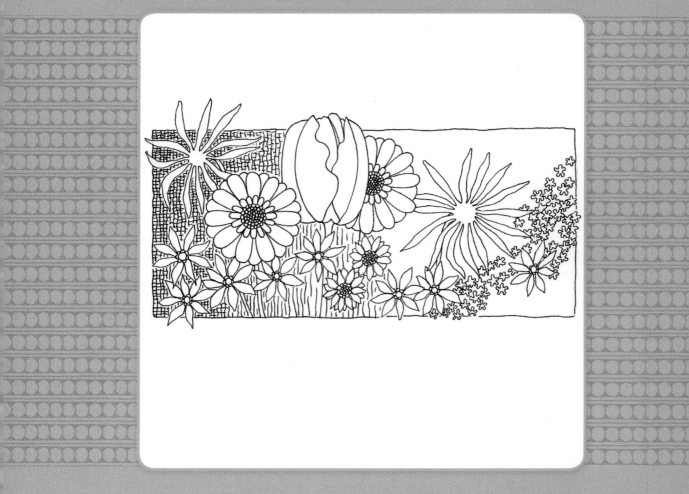

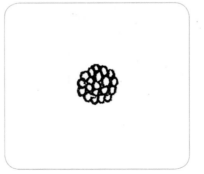

1 Using a pencil, sketch a rectangle 3¼ inches (8cm) tall by 7¼ inches (18cm) wide.

2 With a pen, draw a cluster of very small Os grouped in a circle.

3 Draw a ring of larger Os around the perimeter, and add a ring of U shapes.

Drawing some flowers outside the penciled rectangle creates the illusion of depth.

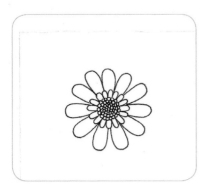

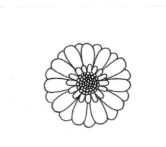

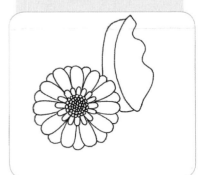

4 Draw a second ring of U shapes, this time larger, for the outer petals.

5 Add a final ring of curved lines that stretch from petal to petal.

6 A tulip adds contrast. Draw the curved lines of a side view of a petal.

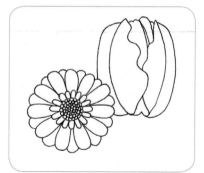

7 Draw the right petal, overlapping and covering most of the rear one.

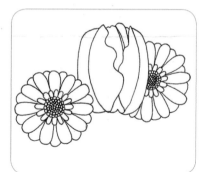

8 Repeat steps 2 through 5 to draw a second flower like the first one overlapped by the tulip.

9 Create a new flower with a wavering, continuous line. Leave the center blank.

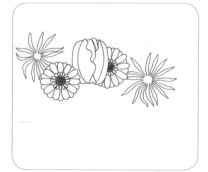

10 Draw another similar flower in the upper-left corner, reaching beyond the frame.

11 Begin a smaller flower with a circle center ringed by half circle petals.

12 Draw this flower's petals, similar to what you did in steps 9 and 10, but make them smaller, pointed, closed shapes.

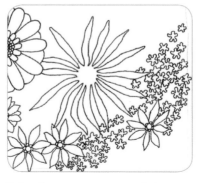

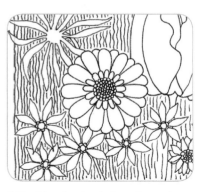

13 Add more of these smaller flowers, arranging them in different-size groups.

14 Draw variations of the daisies, and fill the right side with tiny flower contours.

15 Shade the left side with wavering, vertical lines that stop short of the flowers.

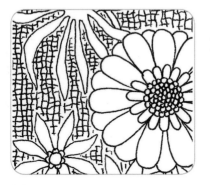

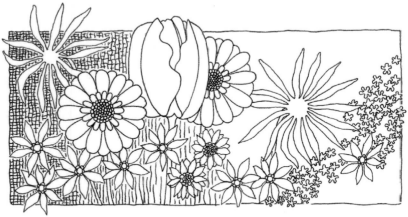

16 Complete the far-left-side shading with short, wavering, horizontal lines that cross step 15's vertical lines.

BIRD

This little ruffed grouse displays a wide range of tangles that are effective when doodling birds. As with most doodles, choose tangles that contrast textures and values to build levels of interest.

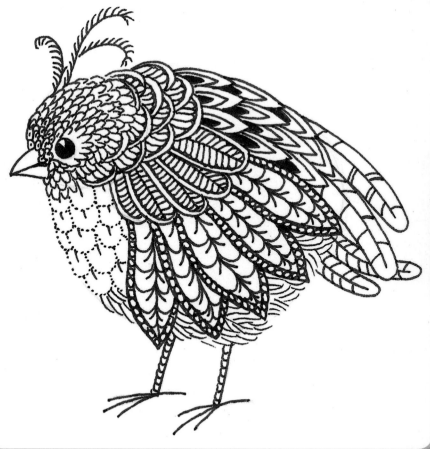

1 Using a pencil, lightly sketch the main shapes and divisions.

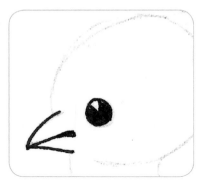

2 Ink the beak. To create the eye, use a shaded circle with a small triangle left uncolored.

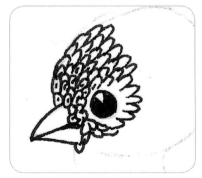

3 Draw dotted ovals near the beak and small U shapes on the crown and around the eye.

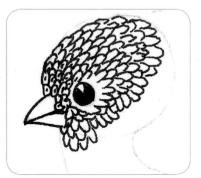

4 Continue drawing slightly larger U shapes at the throat and back of the head, following the contour of the bird's body.

Draw the two curves of this tangle first; then fill with repeating Js.

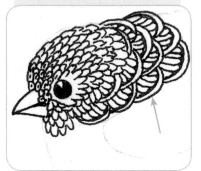

5 Draw demi feathers at the upper back and around to the cheek, rotating the pattern as you work around the bird's body.

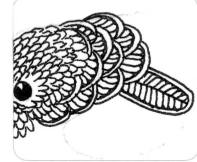

6 Where the demi feathers end, draw a mid-length feather made of two bounding curves and then a midrib line and Js.

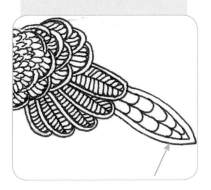

Alternate the direction of the J shapes by starting in the middle and then curving downward and outward.

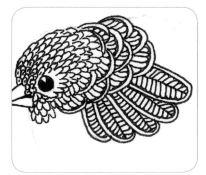

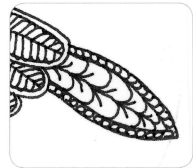

7   Continue the mid-length feathers proceeding downward, arranging them so the previous feathers overlap the new ones.

8   Start a long flight feather with a pointed double boundary and repeating J shapes.

9   Complete the flight feather with small, curved lines and small beading circles.

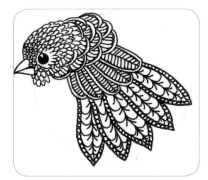

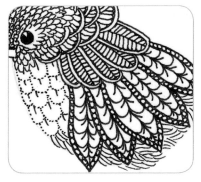

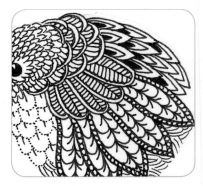

10   Draw more flight feathers that rotate gradually downward.

11   Add the soft chest feathers using dotted Us with short centerlines that transition into curved hatching. Change the direction of the hatch marks occasionally.

12   Create the back feathers with a tangle of repeating, curved Vs with shaded centers.

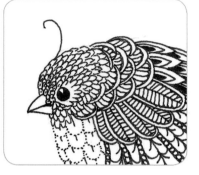

13 Begin a crest feather with a curving line that starts at the head.

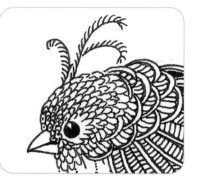

14 Draw barbs projecting from the shaft of the feather, and add crest feathers curving backward.

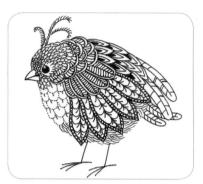

15 Ink in the upper tail feathers and then the lower ones. Draw the legs and feet.

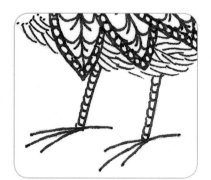

16 Add beading circles on one side of the legs to thicken them.

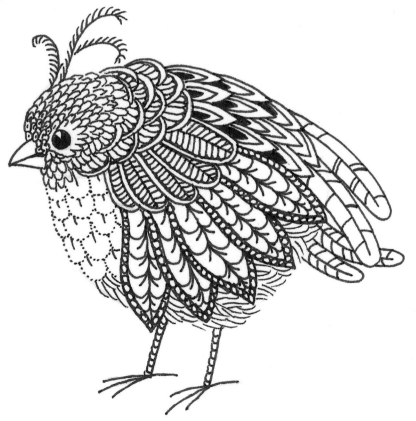

BIRD

CELTIC EVERLASTING KNOT

The Celtic everlasting knot combines repetition, symmetry, and woven patterns. Study these forms to learn their basic overlapping structure.

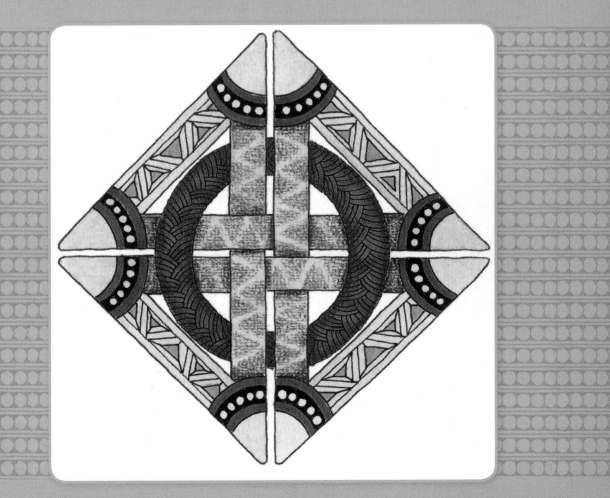

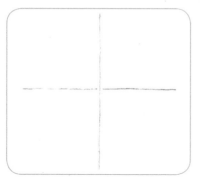

1 Using a pencil, draw a 5-inch (12.5cm) vertical axis line, and cross it at its midpoint with another 5-inch (12.5cm) line, perpendicular to the first.

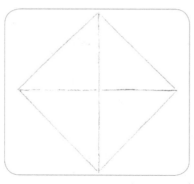

2 Connect the ends of the axes with straight diagonal lines.

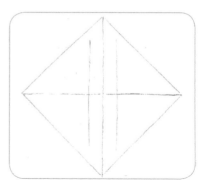

3 Draw two vertical lines about ³⁄₈ inch (1cm) away from the vertical axis.

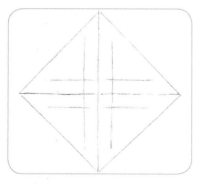

4 Rotate your paper 90 degrees, and repeat step 3.

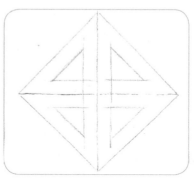

5 Draw four diagonal lines about ³⁄₈ inch (1cm) in from the square's edges.

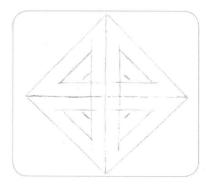

6 Draw four short, slightly curved lines about ⁷⁄₈ inch (2cm) from the center.

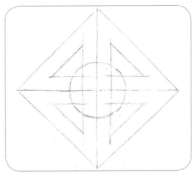

7   Connect the lines from step 6 to make a circle crossing over the horizontal and vertical bars.

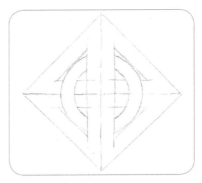

8   Create another circle $^3/_8$ inch (1cm) outside the first, and erase the sections in both circles that pass under the vertical bars.

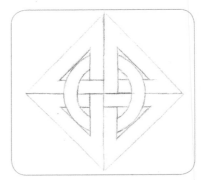

9   Erase sections of the construction lines, and refine the crossing parts so they appear to weave.

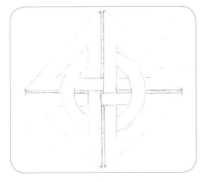

10   Widen the gap of the central axes, and lighten the drawing with a kneaded eraser.

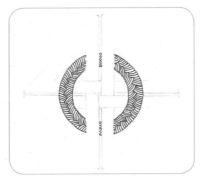

11   Now, using a black pen, fill the ring with the braid tangle and outline the shape.

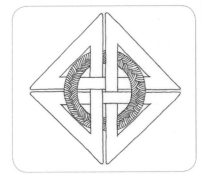

12   Continuing in pen, outline the knot shape.

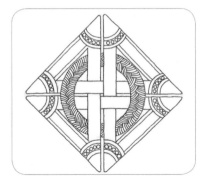

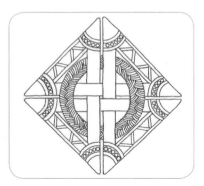

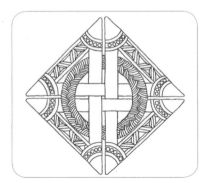

13 Add curving beaded panels in the corners and panel lines to the straight outside sections.

14 Draw double-line Vs in the straight panel sections.

15 Draw a small triangle and radiating corner lines in each of the panel's triangular areas.

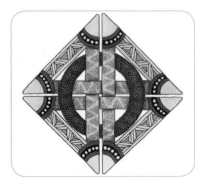

16 Color with black ink, gray and pink watercolors, brown and gray markers, and colored pencils. Shade the ring and woven strips with a pale color and then emphasize the edges and triangles with a darker color.

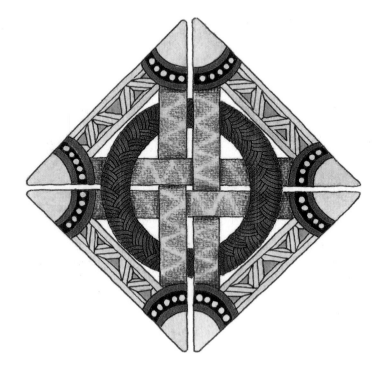

ILLUMINATED LETTER

The medieval illuminated letter was a doorway through which the reader entered the rich fantasy world of imagination. Combine living creatures and nature with letterforms to create your own surprising illumination.

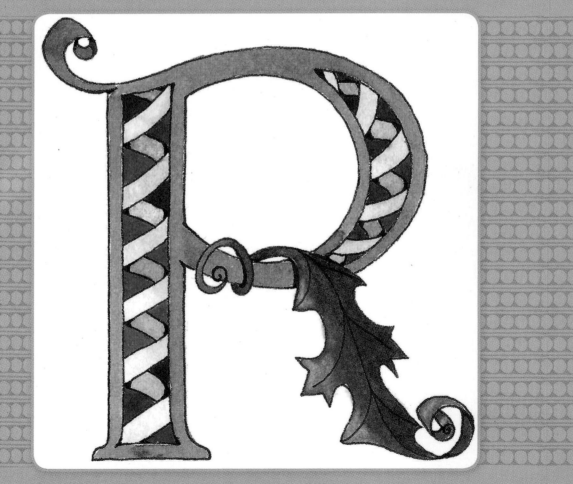

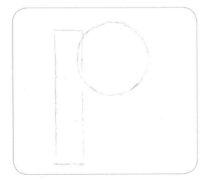

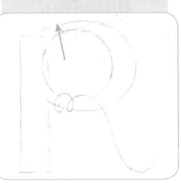

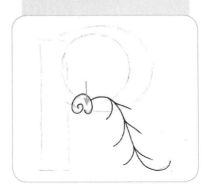

1 Using a pencil, sketch a rectangle ⅝ inches (1.5cm) wide by 3 inches (7.5cm) tall. Then draw a circle 1½ inches (3.8cm) in diameter.

2 Refine the construction with a line that surrounds the circle, and add a downward-looping line.

3 With black ink, trace the looping line in front of the letter and add downward curves for the leaf's veins.

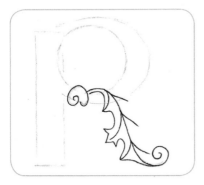

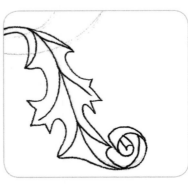

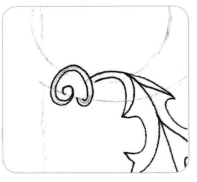

4 Add the curved and pointed left contour of the leaf, and draw the spiral at the tip.

5 Create the right contour to mirror the left side. Complete the spiral with contour lines.

6 Add an interior contour and a small spiraling end to the vine.

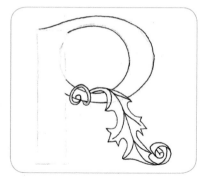

7   Outline the curving bowl of the letter.

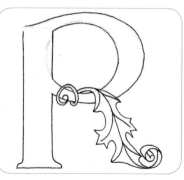

8   Rotate your paper to the left, and draw the upright stem of the letter horizontally.

Draw this line first.

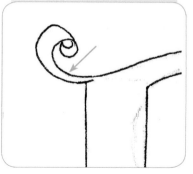

9   Add the curl at the top by drawing the interior spiral first.

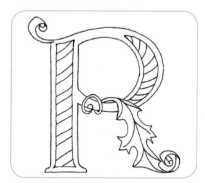

10   Draw two panel contours, and add pairs of faintly curving lines in the interiors.

With black ink, color in the valleys of the curves.

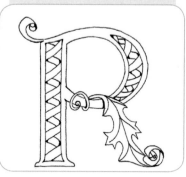

11   Complete the ribbon tangle with contours that link the forward parts.

This gold is a mix of yellow, red, and a very small amount of green.

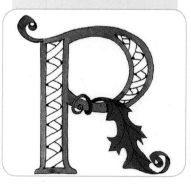

12   Using #4 round brush and watercolors, paint the body of the letter gold, the leaf green, and the vine red.

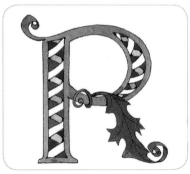

13 Continue with water-colors, painting the interior triangles magenta and the interior ribbon pale violet.

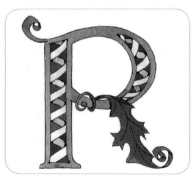

14 Paint the forward sections of ribbon pale pink.

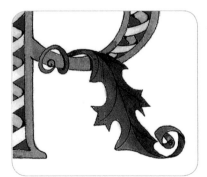

15 Add dark green to the far side of the leaf.

To fill an area with watercolor, paint it with a pale version of the color up to the shape's edge and then add richer color into the wet area with gentle touches. To lift off color, first paint with rich color and let it dry. Then apply water with a small round brush with gentle dabs and lightly blot the area with a paper towel.

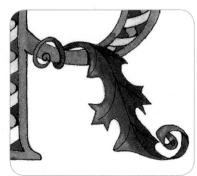

16 Create a highlight by wetting the near leaf tips and then blotting to lift off color.

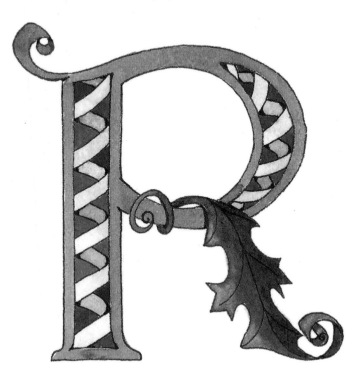

TILING

Doodling tiles often involves designs with reflective balance and dense, repeating color patterns. Think of unusual ways to group shapes with color choices as you draw, and use colored pencils on medium-textured watercolor paper for added depth.

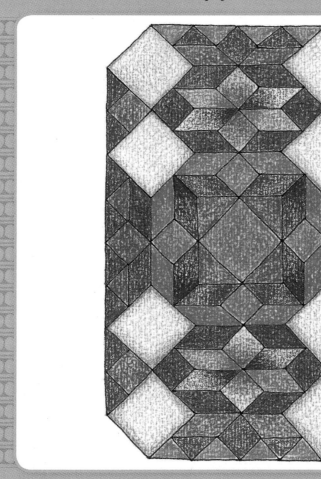

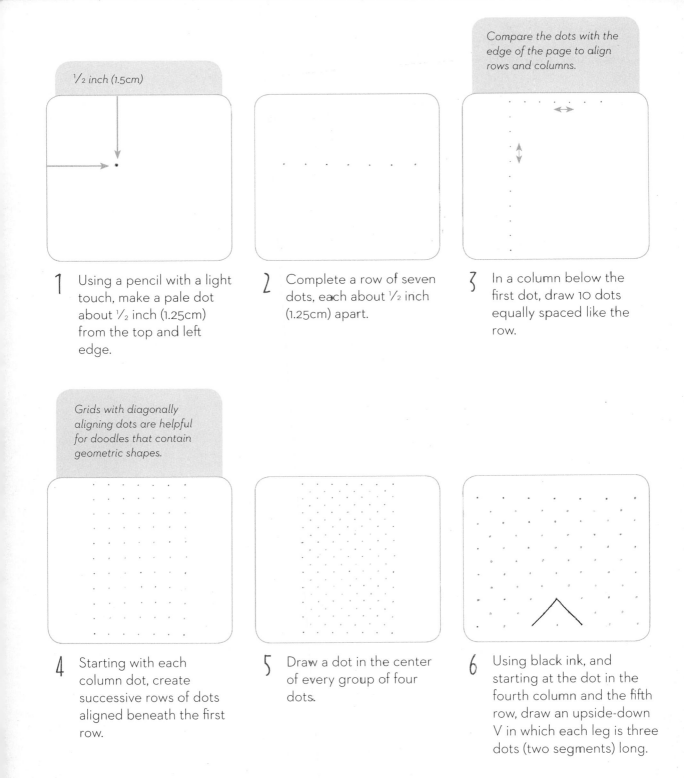

½ inch (1.5cm)

Compare the dots with the edge of the page to align rows and columns.

1 Using a pencil with a light touch, make a pale dot about ½ inch (1.25cm) from the top and left edge.

2 Complete a row of seven dots, each about ½ inch (1.25cm) apart.

3 In a column below the first dot, draw 10 dots equally spaced like the row.

Grids with diagonally aligning dots are helpful for doodles that contain geometric shapes.

4 Starting with each column dot, create successive rows of dots aligned beneath the first row.

5 Draw a dot in the center of every group of four dots.

6 Using black ink, and starting at the dot in the fourth column and the fifth row, draw an upside-down V in which each leg is three dots (two segments) long.

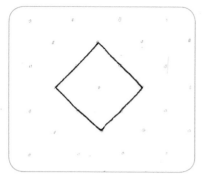

7 Draw another V shape mirroring, and connected to, the previous V, making a diamond shape.

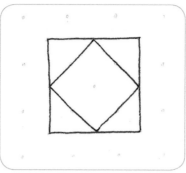

8 Connect dots to make a larger square surrounding the diamond.

Connecting two dots makes one side of these small, slanted squares.

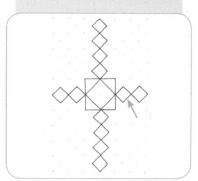

9 Draw small diamonds aligned with the points of the central diamond.

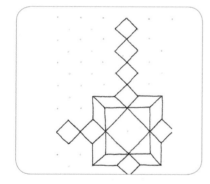

10 Complete the corners of a larger-level square surrounding the previous-level square.

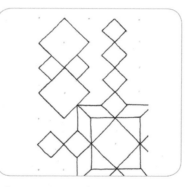

11 Draw two large and two small diamonds in the upper corner.

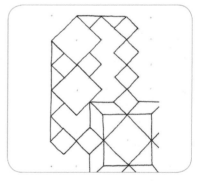

12 Complete the outside edge of the design with short lines.

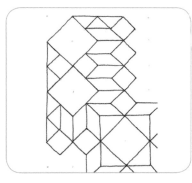

13 Add more lines to create several small parallelograms.

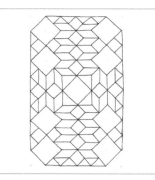

14 In each remaining quadrant of the design, repeat steps 11 through 13 to reflect the completed corner of step 13.

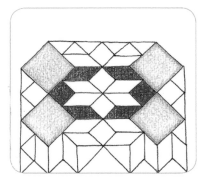

15 Color the large squares light green and the shapes framing the stars dark green. Shade the large diamond to be darker at the edges for emphasis.

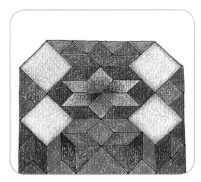

16 Complete the shading with yellow, apple green, turquoise, cobalt blue, purple, and yellow, coloring both halves of the design to reflect.

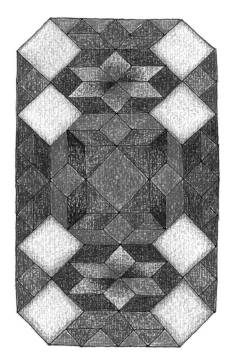

DOODLE WITH SAVED WHITE SPACE

Saving areas of paper to show within a doodle is a fun way to create unity. Here, the white space divides the image so each area can be treated as a unique space while being part of the whole.

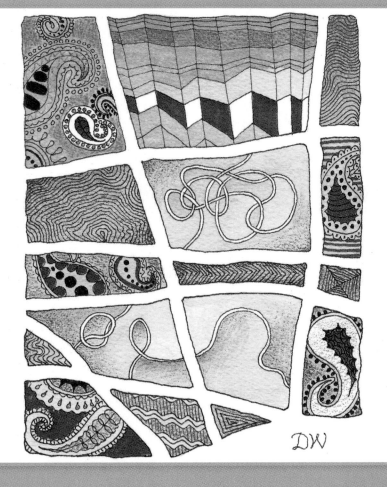

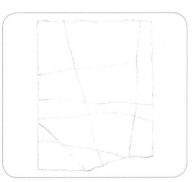

1 Prepare a piece of watercolor paper 6³/₄ inches (17cm) wide by 8¹/₂ inches (22cm) tall.

2 Using a pencil, sketch a rectangle with a piece missing in the lower-right corner.

3 Draw four wavy horizontal lines across the rectangle, angling upward and downward.

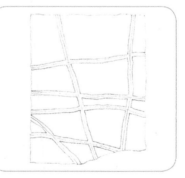

4 Draw three lines that angle downward, crossing the previous lines.

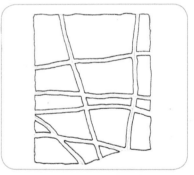

5 Draw shapes set in from the intersecting lines to widen them.

6 Using black ink, trace the new shapes, except for where they overlap, to create the narrow gaps.

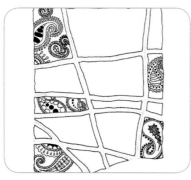

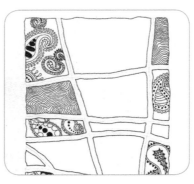

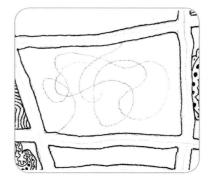

7 Draw a variety of paisley shapes in five alternating side spaces.

8 Create patterns using a contour tangle in two alternating side spaces.

9 Begin drawing loops in a center space by first creating a looping line with your pencil.

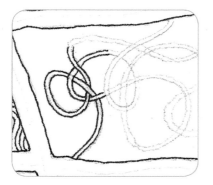

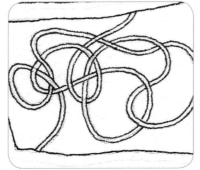

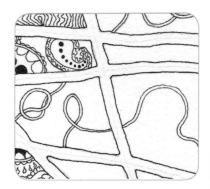

10 Draw another line parallel to the first and then begin tracing the loop contours.

11 Complete the loops by alternating the overlapping sections.

12 Draw more loops in two lower sections that appear to continue from the previous one.

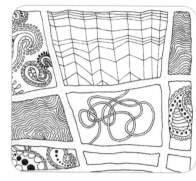

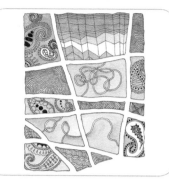

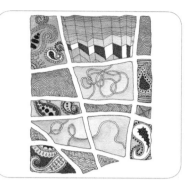

13 Fill the top-middle section with a pleated tangle.

14 Using a #4 round watercolor brush, paint all the sections with pale blue watercolor, leaving some parts unpainted.

15 Color various parts with a brown marker.

The mock deckled edge gives this piece of medium textured watercolor paper added visual appeal. To achieve this handmade paper look, carefully tear the sheet to size and round the corners with scissors.

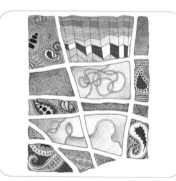

16 Shade shapes and darken corners with turquoise and magenta colored pencils.

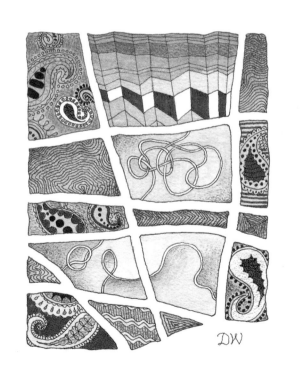

DOODLE WITH SAVED WHITE SPACE

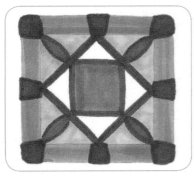

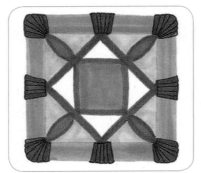

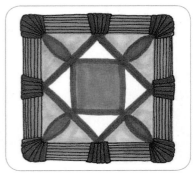

7   Color the areas around the elongated ovals gray. Color the center square light orange.

8   Ink the corners and side gold shapes. Within each of the shapes, draw the texture section by section.

9   Draw repeating lines the length of the spaces between the corner and side shapes.

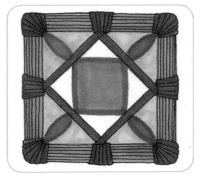

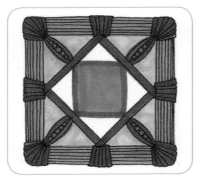

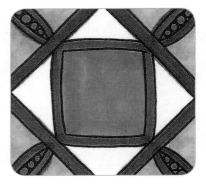

10   Section by section, outline the diamond shape.

11   Draw a beaded shape on the elongated ovals by adding the contours first and then drawing the beads and shading.

12   Outline the center square.

    CHAPTER 11: ASSEMBLING PATTERNS INTO SHAPES

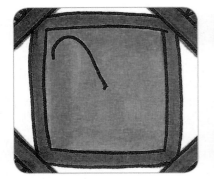

13 Begin the flower form by making a curved question mark shape that ends in the center.

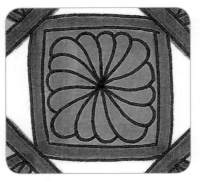

14 Draw more curved shapes rotating around the center.

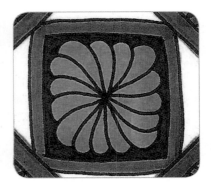

15 Color the space between the flower and the frame black.

Instead of markers, you can use watercolors to color your doodle, but markers won't warp your paper like watercolors could.

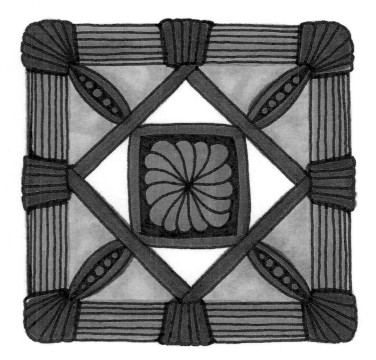

DOODLE WITH COLORED PENCILS

Floating bands are just the visual surprise needed for this ornamental pillow doodle. As used here, colored pencils can shade a base layer before inking, add touches after inking, or shade over marker.

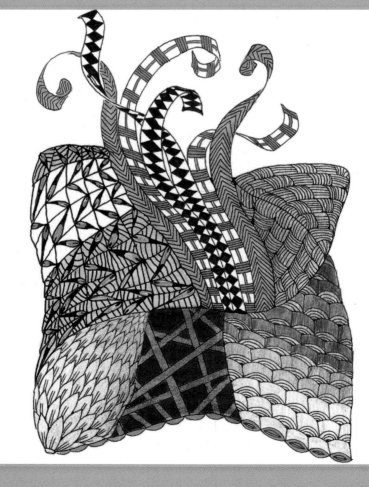
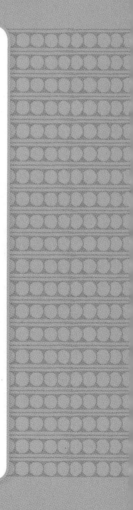

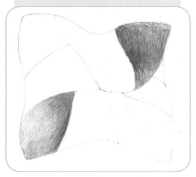

1 Sketch a curved contour main shape with sections, and color two corner shapes with colored pencils.

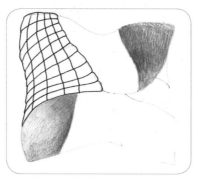

2 Draw a bumpy grid in the upper-left section.

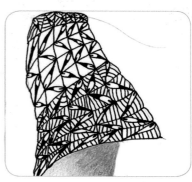

3 Alternate diagonal shapes in the distorted boxes, and add some short shading lines.

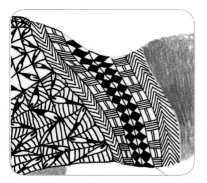

4 Divide the upper-central section by drawing band divisions, and fill them with an assortment of linear tangles.

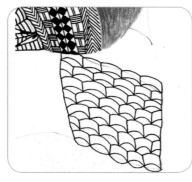

5 Fill the lower-right section with a string of curves, some short verticals, and another string.

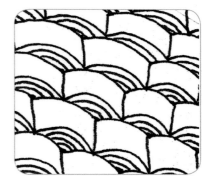

6 Add curves within the smaller curved shapes.

DOODLE WITH COLORED PENCILS

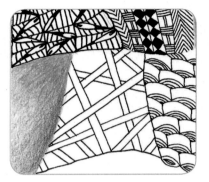

7 Draw overlapping bands in the lower-central section.

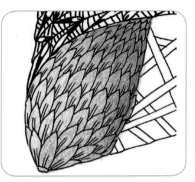

8 Starting at the bottom of the lower-left section, draw a repeating leaf shape with two shading lines in each.

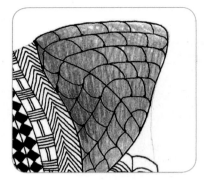

9 Draw a puffy-looking grid in the upper-right section.

For a softer look, leave small gaps where the band turns.

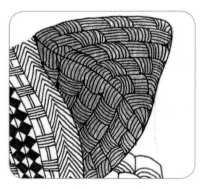

10 Add shading lines to the grid.

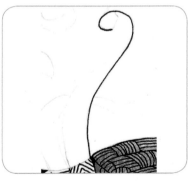

11 Begin the extension of the rightmost band by drawing a long, curved line that begins to spiral at the end.

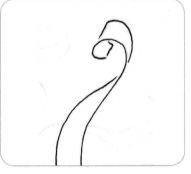

12 Add the left curve and the upper parts.

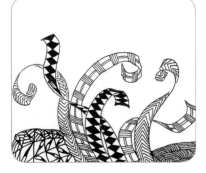

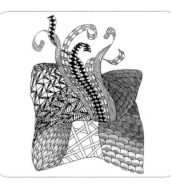

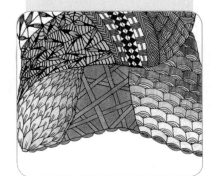

13 Draw the bands in front first and then add the remaining ones.

14 Color the upper-left pattern with yellow and turquoise. In the lower-right area, shade the bottom doodles pale magenta and the tops purple.

15 Extend the scallop along the bottom edge from the lower-right area. With olive green, gray, and gray-blue markers, color the bands section and complete the edging.

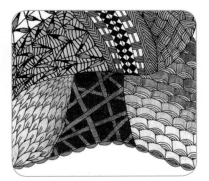

16 Color the entire lower central section lightly with reddish brown and then color the spaces darker.

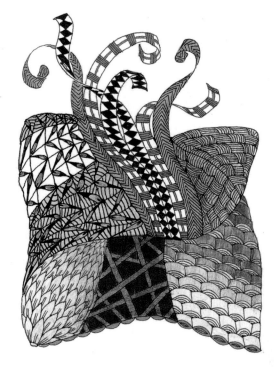

DOODLE WITH SPOT COLOR

Along with being the only colored element, the six-petaled "prima donna" flower of this doodle has fine detail and is situated higher. The leaves support its importance with repeating lines that create contrasting darker value.

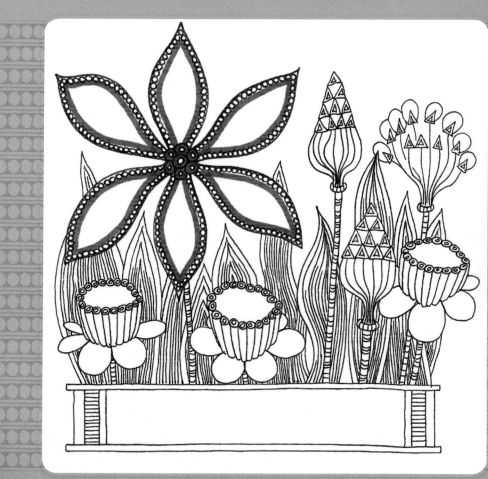

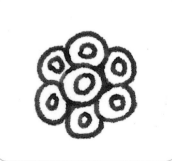

1 With a reddish-brown pen, draw a circle with a small circle inside it and encircle it with six more.

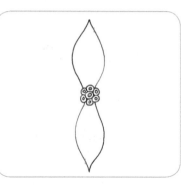

2 Draw two slender curving petals oriented vertically from the circled center.

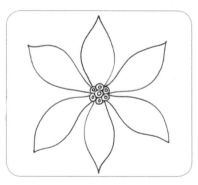

3 Add four more petals oriented diagonally.

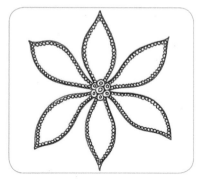

4 Draw beads along the inside edge of the petals.

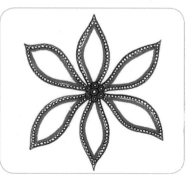

5 With a gold marker, make a line tracing the bead contour, and color the center circles.

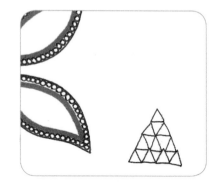

6 To the right of the first flower, begin a flower bud with small triangles set in a triangle formation in black ink.

DOODLE WITH SPOT COLOR

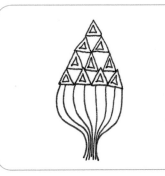

7   Beneath the triangles, draw curving lines that meet to form the base of the flower bud.

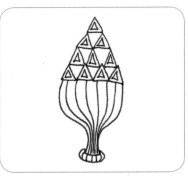

8   Make two horizontally curving lines and short lateral lines to create a ring where the stem meets the flower's base.

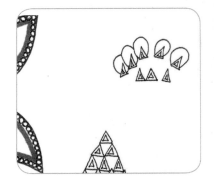

9   Above the previous flower, make another with similar triangles that are spread apart a bit with curves attached to some of them.

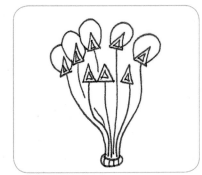

10   Draw lines that curve downward from the triangles to meet at a ring like the one in step 8.

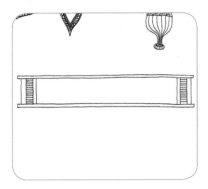

11   Draw a narrow, horizontal box beneath the flowers made of very narrow rectangles and horizontal shading lines.

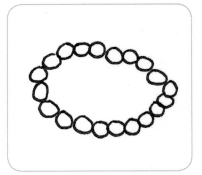

12   Beneath the large flower, draw a ring of small circles.

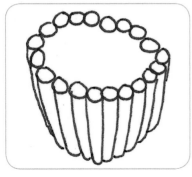

13 From the center circle of the ring at the bottom, draw a tube shape downward and add more tubes to the left and right of it.

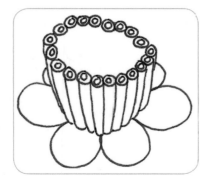

14 Make very small circles in the small circles of the ring, and add circular petals at the base of the flower.

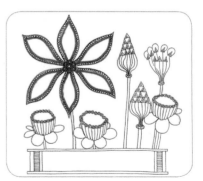

15 Add more flowers, and draw stems made of pairs of lines going from each flower to the box below.

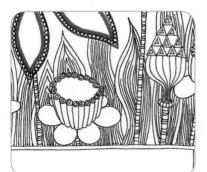

16 Add leaves with repeating curved lines, and add horizontal curved lines to the stems.

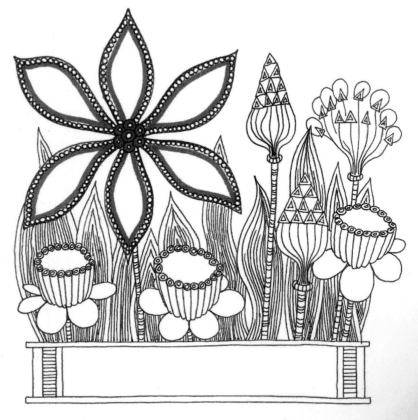

DOODLE WITH SPOT COLOR

12

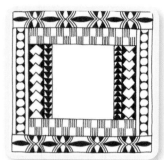

DOODLE SWATCHES

In this chapter, you discover a few more tangles to ponder. Some stress exact proportions while others can be distorted. Pick one, and dive in.

If you haven't yet started a swatch book, begin with these. Grids are often helpful when copying, but when you become familiar with the units and size relationships of a tangle, you can draw many of them freehand. In the beginning, though, feel comfortable copying and collecting them. Be sure to add your own notes and any variations you might come across. As you learn to speak with shapes and pattern, swatches become your visual vocabulary.

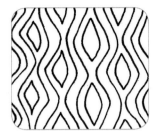

CURVACEOUS

The organic waveforms of this tangle produce even tone, and its gridlike structure can be distorted to gradually grow wider or narrower to fill most areas.

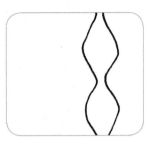

1 In ink, draw a pair of undulating vertical lines that reflect.

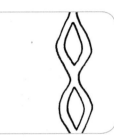

2 Draw shapes that fit in the space between the undulating verticals but leave a small gap.

3 Outside the first pair of undulating verticals, draw two more.

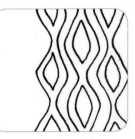

4 Create two more curvaceous tangles that fit next to the first.

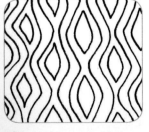

5 Add more of the tangle to make a pattern that fills the desired area.

CHAPTER 12: DOODLE SWATCHES

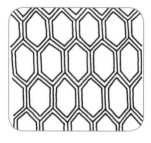

HONEYCOMB

Color, or shade with lines, the centers of the hexagons for alternative versions of this geometric tangle.

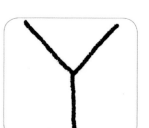

1 In ink, draw a Y with arms spread about 90 degrees.

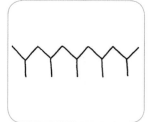

2 Draw four more Y shapes so the ends of their arms connect to create a row.

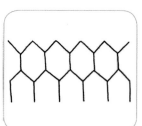

3 Add more Y shapes whose arms connect to the uprights of the first Y shapes.

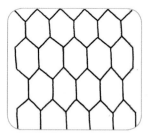

4 Complete four rows of connected Ys.

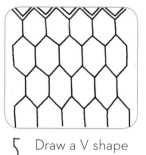

5 Draw a V shape in the empty space between the arms of each Y in the top row.

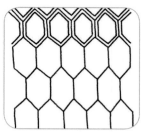

6 Draw a concentric hexagon inside each hexagon in the first row.

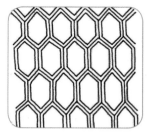

7 Make concentric shapes in all the hexagons and empty spaces.

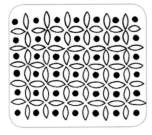

PETALDOT

The contrasting values of the petal shapes and the colored dots create a delicate texture.

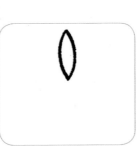

1 In ink, draw a vertically balanced line curving left about ½ inch (1.25cm) tall.

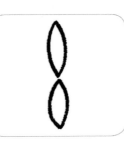

2 Draw a curve that reflects the first and makes a petal shape.

3 Draw another petal shape directly below the first.

4 Draw two horizontally oriented petal shapes to complete one petaldot tangle.

5 Add three petal shapes to make a petaldot tangle that joins the first one.

6 Add four more sets of three petal groups to make a row of the tangle.

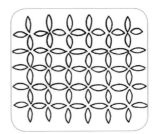

7 Create four more rows of the tangle by adding petals onto the first row of tangles.

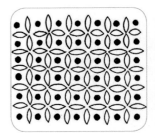

8 Complete the pattern by adding a dot in the center of each void.

CHAPTER 12: DOODLE SWATCHES

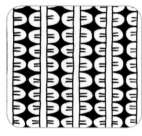

BEANPOLE

The colored negative spaces and repeating bumps with stripes produce a bold pattern.

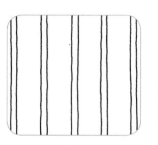

1 In ink, draw five pairs of parallel vertical lines freehand in ink $3/8$ inch (1cm) apart.

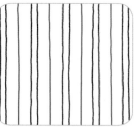

2 Draw a vertical guideline down the center of each space between the pairs of lines.

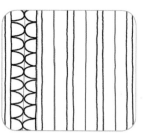

3 Draw a column of repeating curves between the left side of the first space and the guidelines added in step 2.

4 Draw a column of curves that reflect the first on the opposite side of the space.

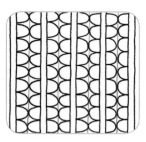

5 Fill the remaining spaces with curves like steps 3 and 4.

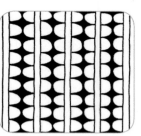

6 Color the spaces between the columns of curves black.

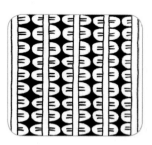

7 Make pairs of short black lines in the curved shapes.

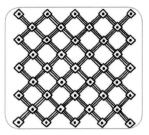

LATTICE

You can draw this fun tangle rotated so the diagonals become verticals and horizontals.

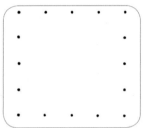

1 In ink, draw a frame of dots about ⅝ inch (1.5cm) apart, using a ruler as a guide to evenly space the dots.

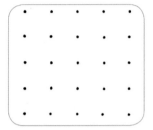

2 Fill the interior of the frame with evenly spaced dots that align with the previous dots.

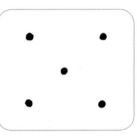

3 Draw a dot in the center of the upper-left group of four dots.

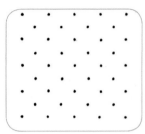

4 Draw a dot in the center of every group of four dots made in steps 1 and 2.

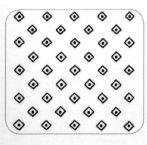

5 Draw a diamond around every dot.

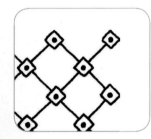

6 Draw a line that connects each diamond and so it aligns with the dots.

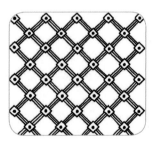

7 Draw a line on each side of the center connecting line.

CHAPTER 12: DOODLE SWATCHES

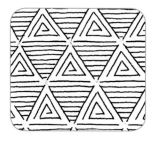

PYRAMID

This tangle creates very even tone with a dynamic turn.

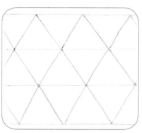

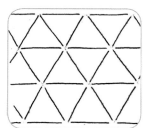

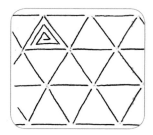

1 Using a pencil, draw four freehand parallel guidelines about ½ inch (1.25cm) apart and about 3 inches (7.5cm) long.

2 Draw freehand Vs so the ends align with the points of the next row.

3 Ink the triangles, leaving a gap at the corners.

4 Draw an angular spiral in the upper-left triangle that's pointing up.

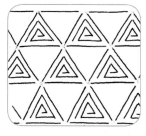

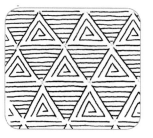

5 Fill all the upward-pointing triangles with angular spirals.

6 Shade the downward-pointing triangles with horizontal lines.

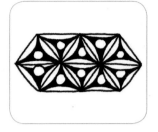

STARSPICE

This tangle is based on the anise seedpod and produces a spicy geometric pattern.

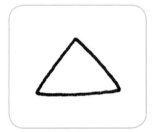 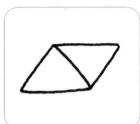 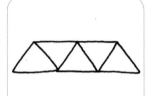 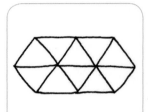

1 Draw a triangle.

2 Create another triangle by drawing a horizontal line and then a diagonal one.

3 Make three more triangles by drawing diagonal and horizontal lines that connect to the previous triangle.

4 Create more triangles that reflect the top row.

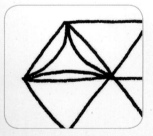 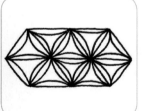 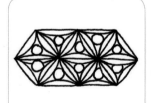 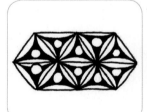

5 Draw curves stretching from corner to corner in the top left triangle.

6 Add curves to all the triangles, and draw only two curves in one of the triangles.

7 Draw small circles in the triangles then add small curves in the triangle with only two curves.

8 With black ink, color the small triangular spaces around the circles.

CHAPTER 12: DOODLE SWATCHES

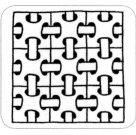

LACED UP

⟨ʔ⊘ʔ•⊘ʔ⟩

With its overlaps, weaves, and gaps, this quirky tangle is full of potential for inventing new designs.

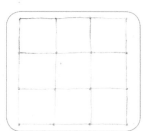

1 Using a pencil, make four rows of four dots spaced ½ inch (1.25cm) apart, and connect them with lines.

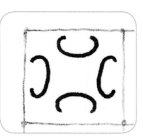

2 In the upper-left box, ink four C shapes, each facing the center of one of the box's sides.

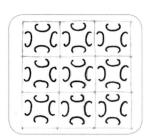

3 Repeat step 2 in all the boxes.

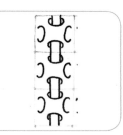

4 In the left three boxes, draw pairs of lines that appear to run the entire length of the grid.

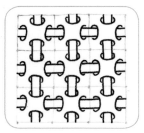

5 Next draw the pairs of lines described in step 4 running down and across all the boxes.

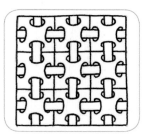

6 Ink the lines of the grid that aren't overlapped by the laces.

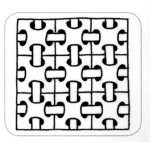

7 Shade the remaining spaces inside the Cs black.

13

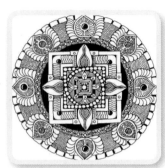

INSPIRATION GALLERY

Inspiration is a seed. Like the center of a mandala, it's the first mark, the center around which everything else is built. All the raw materials for an idea can be right in front of you, but until inspiration unlocks the insight to put it all together, you might feel blocked and not know what to do.

The doodles in this chapter are here to give you inspiration and a few more possibilities of what Zen doodling can be. Don't be afraid to just draw a shape and see what happens. Sometimes all it takes is making a small starting point and then adding the next mark.

FANTASIA

Recognizable naturalistic forms, like butterflies and leaves, sometimes provide an entry to understanding a doodle. However, to the doodler, sometimes they're only forms to fill with pattern. Contrast of patterned areas and white space is one of the visual games being played throughout this doodle.

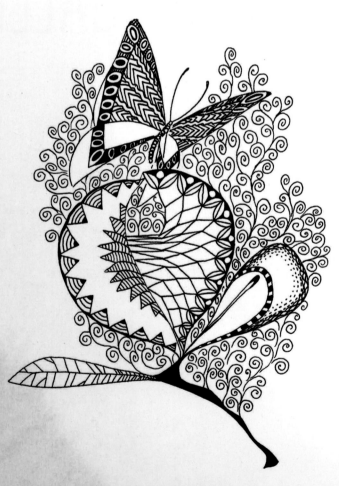

CHAOS

The challenge of this doodle was to create a circuitous path for a dot to travel. The illusion of depth occurs with change of size and overlapping. Pattern still is the main focus, and even the more blank areas have a somewhat asymmetrical shape that lends to the appearance of this Rube Goldberg contraption.

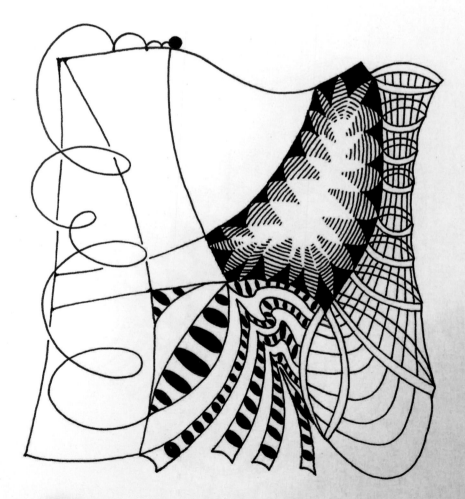

FLOTSAM

Fields of repeating motifs can create a flowing look when made with a curved grid. The wavelike trails of dots and bubbles also suggest a maritime theme. The possibility of multiple readings welcomes the viewer to interpret the forms from many points of view. In this doodle, contrast is found in different patterns and a wide range of tones to create a focal point, rhythm, and balance.

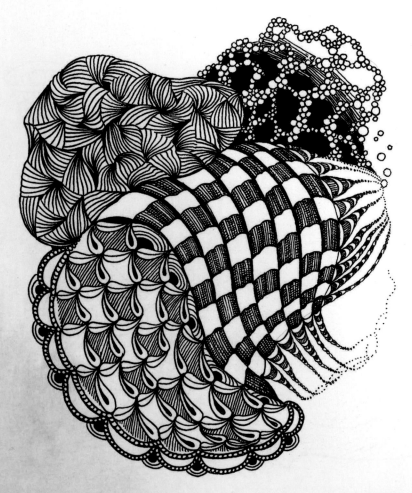

CHAPTER 13: INSPIRATION GALLERY

CATERPILLAR GARDEN

The subject matter suggested by the title of this doodle is recognizable, possibly, by small details like grass and leaf tangles, and the contour and patterns that meander like a crawling caterpillar. Finding these and other elements that support a theme suggested by the title is some of the fun of looking at a doodle.

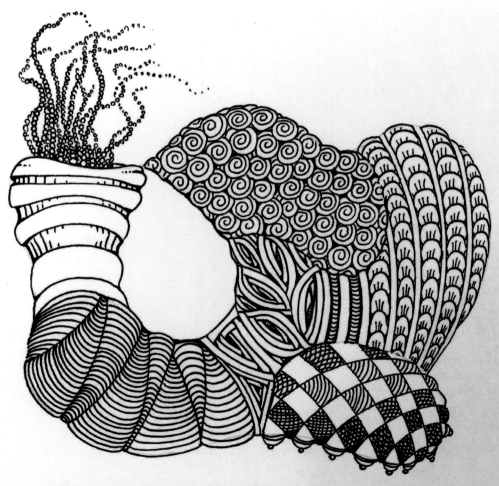

INDEX